MW01505871

No Matter What

No Matter What

90 Devotions for Experiencing
UNEXPECTED JOY
in Tough Times

Jill Baughan

Our Daily Bread
Publishing.

No Matter What: 90 Devotions for Experiencing Unexpected Joy in Tough Times
© 2025 by Jill Baughan

All rights reserved.

Requests for permission to quote from this book should be directed to: Permissions Department, Our Daily Bread Publishing, PO Box 3566, Grand Rapids, MI 49501; or contact us by email at permissionsdept@odb.org.

Published in association with Books & Such Literary Management, www.booksandsuch.com.

Scripture quotations, unless otherwise indicated, are taken from the Holy Bible, New International Version®, NIV®. Copyright © 1973, 1978, 1984, 2011 by Biblica, Inc.™ Used by permission of Zondervan. All rights reserved worldwide. www.zondervan.com.

Scripture quotations marked ESV are taken from the ESV® Bible (The Holy Bible, English Standard Version®), copyright © 2001 by Crossway, a publishing ministry of Good News Publishers. Used by permission. All rights reserved.

Scripture quotations marked MSG are taken from *The Message*, copyright © 1993, 2002, 2018 by Eugene H. Peterson. Used by permission of NavPress. All rights reserved. Represented by Tyndale House Publishers.

Scripture quotations marked NASB are taken from the New American Standard Bible®, copyright © 1960, 1971, 1977, 1995, 2020 by The Lockman Foundation. Used by permission. All rights reserved. lockman.org.

Scripture quotations marked NLT are taken from the *Holy Bible*, New Living Translation, copyright © 1996, 2004, 2015 by Tyndale House Foundation. Used by permission of Tyndale House Publishers, Carol Stream, Illinois 60188. All rights reserved.

Interior design by Michael J. Williams

ISBN: 978-1-64070-396-4

Library of Congress Cataloging-in-Publication Data Available

Printed in the United States of America
25 26 27 28 29 30 31 32 / 8 7 6 5 4 3 2 1

Contents

Part Four: The Best of Life

Introduction

What's it like to be you right now?

You may be sailing along in a cloud of bliss, but more likely you're girding up your loins to face some challenge that elicits a "No thanks, I'd rather not" from your heart.

If that's you, please know this: Right alongside those tough times of yours, joy is walking, just waiting to be discovered—*joy* defined as "deep delight that feeds your soul."

This is your invitation to journey with me, and by the end of this book, I hope you'll feel as though you've had ninety days of encouragement from a good friend—with a sense of humor. Because you need one of those. And God has one to share.

So as we travel together, my friend, may you come to know that your sorrow shouldn't be denied, but neither should it be your address. And when the challenges of life threaten to send your spirit underground, may these pages give you hope for soul-filling delight . . .

First thing in the morning when your feet hit the floor.

Last thing at night before your head hits the pillow.

Or during the day when you need a bit of encouragement from our God, who hears your heart and reminds you that if you go looking for joy, you will most likely find it. No matter what.

PART ONE

The Wonder Years

Focus on Joy

Summing it all up, friends, I'd say you'll do best by filling
your minds and meditating on things true, noble, reputable,
authentic, compelling, gracious—the best, not the worst; the
beautiful, not the ugly; things to praise, not things to curse.
—Philippians 4:8 MSG

When I was a child, the Tilt-A-Whirl at my hometown's annual street fair taught me this life-changing truth: it is entirely possible for a human being to laugh and throw up at the same time.

In that crazy space, I discovered that in order to experience the extreme thrill of the ride, I had to do some heavy-duty focusing on the joyful delirium of being enthusiastically hurled around in circles.

Little did I know that years later, when I was a grown-up, God would use this revelation to show me—on a deeper level—that joy and sorrow can occupy the same space, that they can walk (or hurl) alongside each other on the same road. We just have to be intentional about drawing from the joy while we're going through the tough stuff.

Now obviously, focusing our thoughts on joy is often counter-intuitive; it doesn't make our challenges disappear, and it doesn't make us hurt less.

But a little mental discipline can determine the trajectory of our hearts.

I know—mental discipline sounds like low-carb thinking. No fun, no joy. But as author Tommy Newberry says, "Though God's grace doesn't demand mental discipline, living a life of joyful excellence must be preceded by it."*

In other words, when it comes to deep delight that feeds your soul, you are not at the mercy of your circumstances. You have the choice to direct your mind's focus toward joy.

And that, my friend, is very good news.

A PRAYER

Dear God, sometimes it's hard to focus on delight when life is spinning out of control around me. Please make me aware of even the small joys that walk alongside my difficulties.

---

* Tommy Newberry, *The Daily Guide to a Joy-Filled Life: Living the 4:8 Principle* (Carol Stream, IL: Tyndale, 2021), 83.

2

Grab Your Blankie

I am leaving you with a gift—peace of mind and
heart. And the peace I give is a gift the world
cannot give. So don't be troubled or afraid.

—John 14:27 NLT

Recently I went to a football practice where my six-year-old grandson was playing. When he ran over to the sidelines to get a drink of water, I held up my phone camera and said, "Hey, good boy! Give me your game face!"

And did he ever.

He looked for all the world like he was about fifteen.

Tough. All business. Git 'er done.

The next day, I took him to the movies. As we settled in with our drinks and popcorn, the lights went down, and after a couple minutes, I heard him say to himself, "I shoulda brought my blankie. It's dark in here. My blankie makes me feel better."

I'll admit, I had to chuckle as I put my arm around him.

But then I thought, "Oh, aren't we *all* six-year-olds, with a game face one day, looking all tough and stuff, and then needing our blankies the next to make us feel better in the dark?"

When the unknown looms ahead and leaves us unable to see, we search for some peace, even as adults.

And when you can't locate your hand in front of your game face because it's so dark around you, it helps to remember that God is right there with you, offering the comfort of himself—a "blankie" of the very best kind.

A PRAYER

Dear God, when my life is full of uncertainty and I start to panic because I can't see what's ahead, please remind me that I don't have to know the circumstances. I only have to settle into your always-there care.

3

Offer Your Best

Blessed are the pure in heart, for they will see God.
—Matthew 5:8

What's the most disappointing gift you've ever received? And exactly how did you receive it?

Some people are really bad at hiding their amusement, dismay, disgust, or disbelief. These people should take a cue from my mom.

Her birthday was December 4, and when I was a child, I thought the most wonderful birthday present I could give her was a corsage that she could wear during the Christmas season.

Year after year, I "blessed" her with corsages made of fake snowmen, fake poinsettias, and tiny, goofy-eyed elves. I was proudest, though, the year I found a corsage with a disproportionately large aluminum snow shovel in the middle.

I remember being absolutely ecstatic at the thought of my mom parading around all December with a snow shovel pinned to her chest.

But you know, she accepted my offering like it was a diamond from Tiffany's because she loved the heart of the giver.

Fortunately for us, God too accepts our gifts to Him—our sometimes awkward, bumbling, and even failed attempts to serve Him and each other.

The music we make might have mistakes or need some serious Auto-Tune assistance.

Our acts of service may not be enough to take away the pain or fully meet the need.

Our words, spoken or written, are often not elegant or even adequate.

But God's sight goes past our limited perspective and straight into the pure heart of the giver.

And there is such joy in knowing that when we give the finest we have, He not only sees us but we see Him right back.

A PRAYER

Dear God, sometimes I feel as though what I have to offer you and others is so inadequate. Thank you for knowing my heart and reassuring me that when I offer the best that's in me, you smile.

4

Look through the Eyes of Your Childhood

The whole earth is filled with awe at your
wonders; where morning dawns, where evening
fades, you call forth songs of joy.

—Psalm 65:8

When I was a child, I occasionally spent the night with my Grandma Ellis. Her humble little house was magical—especially the small bedroom where she kept her deep freeze. It never occurred to me that housing a freezer in the bedroom was the slightest bit out of the ordinary, but you know—kids. In fact, I thought it was very cool because in that freezer you could *always* find frozen Milky Way candy bars.

When I visited, I of course slept near the unlimited supply of midnight snacks.

The kitchen had a slightly tilted floor, which never bothered me in the least because that kitchen also contained a short Crown refrigerator perpetually stocked with little glass bottles of Coca-Cola. And somewhere in the kitchen there was also a secret place that regularly gave birth to legions of tiny Tootsie Rolls. Grandma Ellis never ran out of this stuff.

But my favorite parts of her house were the dark green shades that hung at each window. At night, when she pulled them down, the design on each one looked to me like a canvas of twinkling stars against a night sky. I used to stare at them, mesmerized, thinking they really did look like diamonds.

It wasn't until I was an adult that I realized those stars in the night sky came from the farm light outside shining through holes and cracks in the old, worn-out shades.

Friend, can you too access the eyes of your childhood self? Eyes that see unanticipated wonder in the ordinary and heavenly bodies in the holes and cracks of life?

I'll bet you can if you try.

A PRAYER

Dear God, I know that joy is all around, especially in the humble places. Please help me look for it with childlike eyes.

5

Know Who You Really Are

Oh LORD, you have searched me and known me!
—Psalm 139:1 ESV

Did anyone ever call you a hurtful name when you were a child? I thought so.

I was a tall kid, so I was an easy target for Tommy in kindergarten. He insisted on calling me Big Truck all year, which made me feel resentful and insecure—not to mention super ticked off.

A few years later, in the third grade, I was playing kickball on the playground. My athletic prowess was not fully developed yet, so it was no surprise when Butch pitched me the ball and I, running up with intent to nail the thing with all my might, actually missed it altogether, my dress blowing up in my face.

Butch couldn't resist calling this to the attention to everyone in earshot by yelling, "Hey, Big Panties! You missed!"

Obviously, I have not forgotten this insensitive characterization of my underwear.

Then when I was in the fifth grade, my older brother introduced me to one of his high school teachers: "This is my little sister. She's in the fifth grade." To which said teacher replied, "Fifth grade? She's bigger than my wife!"

Big Truck. Big Panties. Bigger Than My Wife. The pattern was not lost on me.

I thought of myself as "Big" for years, even after all my classmates caught up to my height.

Maybe you too have been labeled unfairly or inaccurately by others or even yourself, whether in childhood or adulthood, in a way that doesn't describe you at all.

If so, it helps to counter these lies with the truth: you, my friend, were created and are loved by the God of the universe. And no label can rob you of that reality.

A PRAYER

Dear God, please help me find courage to delight in the truth that you know who I really am, and you created me for joy.

6

Be like Jesus

As we have opportunity, let us do good to all people,
especially to those who belong to the family of believers.

—Galatians 6:10

My friend Glenn was hit by a train.

An excellent golfer at twelve years old, he was at a tournament right next to a set of railroad tracks. He said, "The best golfer in the state was getting ready to putt. I was on the tracks, trying to watch him hit, and I didn't want to make too much noise. I heard the train, but it sounded far away."

However, it was closer than he thought, and the train, traveling at sixty miles per hour, hit him, throwing him twenty-five feet in the air. He was rushed into surgery for five hours to save his life, then placed in the hospital for four months and released on crutches.

Then one January day, Glenn was sitting on a sled in his front yard when a driver lost control of a car on the icy street, plowed through the yard, and hit him.

Again he was rushed to the hospital for surgery, again his life was spared, and again he was in traction in the hospital for three months and released in a wheelchair.

What made him so resilient?

He says if it hadn't been for his faith in Jesus, the whole healing process would have been harder. And I have no doubt, because in his story, I'm thinking Jesus looked a lot like . . .

every nurse who played cards with him to pass the time

every person who paid him a visit

every kid on his baseball team who came to take a team picture in his hospital room

And maybe, for someone else in need, like you and me.

A PRAYER

Dear God, I know several people who have landed in unfortunate places. Please show me how I can be like Jesus to help make their healing process a little easier.

7

Accept Forgiveness

If we confess our sins, he is faithful and just and will forgive us.

—1 John 1:9

I started messing up at a very young age.

When I was six years old, I loved Dum Dum suckers and habitually sneaked them into the living room, where I watched TV. Knowing I would get in trouble for my contraband food, I had to be creative in hiding the evidence.

One day I had the bright idea to put the wrappers and sticks on the back of a full-length mirror that hung in my parents' bedroom, located right off the living room. Brilliant.

Of course my mom, who had the annoying habit of cleaning house on the regular, found them one day, told my father, and they confronted my brother and me.

Neither of us confessed, and to my surprise, my father simply said, "Okay," and let us both go.

I was relieved at first, but all day, I was so jittery that at the sight of him I once threw my hands in the air like I'd been caught robbing a bank, and shouted, "I didn't do it, honest!"

I think this is what tipped him off. Still he said nothing.

Finally, late in the day, I walked into the kitchen where my parents were sitting, to confess. But when he saw me, he sat me in his lap and whispered into my ear, "Why don't you tell Mommy it was you who put those sucker sticks behind the mirror?"

I cried tears of relief, sobbing that I deserved to go to jail. Fortunately, doing time wasn't warranted, just a cleanup. It was considerable work, but my relationship with my father was right again, and that's what really mattered.

So like the gift God offers us.

A PRAYER

Dear God, please help me learn the childlike art of leaning into your forgiveness—even if it comes with a mess to clean up.

8

Pray Out Loud

Devote yourselves to prayer, being watchful and thankful.
— Colossians 4:2

Prayer in the presence of others can be daunting when other people are actually listening.

When my husband was a little boy, he was in a churchwide prayer meeting. Although he was only seven, somehow he already had the idea that, in a roomful of people, silence in the presence of the Almighty was undesirable. So when everyone bowed their heads and closed their eyes, and nothing happened—not one person was offering up any sound whatsoever—he decided to take the prayer bull by the horns. "Oh, Lord!" he fairly shouted, "bless aaall the nations of the earth!"

Well, at least the attendees weren't silent anymore. They were so busy muffling their laughter, nobody could pray with any dignity. And still no one was lifting petitions up.

So Ben tried again. "Oh, Lord!" his little voice bounced off the sanctuary walls. "Bless *aaall* the nations of the earth!"

I think they had to let everybody go after that, since prayer was pretty much a lost cause.

The pressure to fill dead air in the name of Jesus can start when we're very young, and it may continue into adulthood.

Maybe you feel this discomfort yourself. Or perhaps you believe your words are clumsy or inadequate, and listeners are thinking, "So awkward. Land the plane, already."

But don't listen to that lie, because corporate prayer can be a source of joy for someone who needs encouragement.

We can tell people we'll pray for them when they're going through a terrible time, and of course that's encouraging. But encouragement turns into soul massage when we say, "Can I pray for you right now?" and that other person actually *hears* simple, honest words offered to God on his or her behalf.

A PRAYER

Dear God, please let me know when my audible words to you can comfort someone in need. And remind me that nobody—including you—cares about fancy. Only heart.

9

Make Some Mischief

A glad heart makes a cheerful face.
—Proverbs 15:13 ESV

Sometimes mischief can be a gift.

I learned this from watching my parents when I was very young. My mom and dad were part of a group of friends who got together in a rather unconventional manner.

Every now and then they would gather at 5:00 a.m. on a Saturday, call someone they all knew, and all but yell into the phone, "Hey! Good morning! We've got breakfast. See you at your house in five minutes!" Then they—and all of their children—would show up at the door with doughnuts and coffee.

Somehow, it became a demonstration of love to get breakfast bombed like this.

It's so true that "a cheerful heart is good medicine" (Proverbs 17:22). You have to be careful, though.

A couple I know (we'll call them Jack and Diane) decided it would be funny to give their friends, the Crocketts, a sponge cake—made out of a real sponge. They cut it to look like a cake, iced it up, and gave it to their buddies as a gift.

However.

The Crocketts had friends who had recently experienced a

death in their family, and they decided to save themselves a little work by taking the gifted cake to the bereaved.

When Jack and Diane hadn't heard from the Crocketts in a while, they called them and asked if they had enjoyed their "cake." Whereupon the Crocketts sheepishly confessed they had actually passed it on to their grieving friends.

Cue the uh-ohs.

Of course the Crocketts had to explain their faux pas to the mourners, who were most gracious—if not a little confused—and who had to laugh, even in the middle of their sorrow.

So tell me, friend—do you know someone who could use a smile brought on by a good-natured shenanigan? Someone who needs to know that you love them enough to make them laugh?

A PRAYER

Dear God, I pray that you would show me how to shower a little unorthodox attention on some unsuspecting soul who needs some extra joy.

10

Celebrate Today's Sweetness

Celebrate God all day every day. I mean, revel in him!
—Philippians 4:4 MSG

I know. You have a lot on your mind.

And sometimes all that's on your mind keeps you from recognizing and celebrating the delights that appear in your path every day, just waiting to be enjoyed.

It's so easy to let today's cares and busyness keep us from embracing its joys. We'd all do well to remember the story author Beth Levine tells of her little boy. One day, she says, "our son decided that not only was underwear objectionable, the rest of his clothes were as well. I found him running around the house stark naked, only pausing long enough to grab a treat from the kitchen table.

"'Mama!' he cried with soul-soaring glee. 'I'm naked! Naked with CANDY!'"

"What more can you ask from life?" Beth asked her husband. "I feel like being naked with candy myself."*

*Beth Levine, "Mr. Wonderful," *Woman's Day*, February 18, 1997, 144.

And to that I say, "We should *all* aspire to be exactly that."

Well, maybe if we redefine our terms here.

What if you thought of *naked* as the freedom to be your authentic, God-created self, and *candy* as anything sweet in your life, just waiting for you to pick it up and revel in it?

What if you made a conscious effort to proactively search for the joyful confections that God is offering this day—even if this day happens to be perfectly awful?

What if you brought your whole authentic self to a table loaded with treats and lived "naked with candy" all the rest of your days?

A PRAYER

Dear God, thank you for offering up sweet gifts even in tough times. Please help me to recognize them, scoop them up, and celebrate them with "soul-soaring glee"!

Do a Little Thing

If you give even a cup of cold water to one of the least
of my followers, you will surely be rewarded.

—Matthew 10:42 NLT

Little things can sometimes make a big, amazing difference.

My grandfather was a humble man with a humble job: he drove a road grader, smoothing out gravel roads in rural Indiana. But everyone on his route knew him because he did something extra on his job—a little thing that spread a lot of joy.

If you are of a certain age, you may remember Chiclets from your childhood—little white squares of candy-coated gum that came in a small yellow box.

Grandpa bought them by the case—but not for himself. He took them on his rounds every day, and whenever he saw people—especially children—in the yard, he would throw Chiclets out the window for them to run and gather up.

Which seems like a very little, forgettable thing to do.

But over sixty years later, a man named Bill remembers the extreme kindness of my grandpa. One morning his mother told him and his two siblings that they were going into town, so they'd be gone when the Grader Man drove by, lobbing little pieces of joy at them. They didn't want to miss that! They loudly protested, but their mom insisted that they go. So off they trudged, cranky when they left and when they arrived back home.

Until.

Their mom went out to the mailbox, opened it, and found three tiny white squares of gum waiting for the three children who missed the treat-hurling Grader Man's rounds that day.

A Chiclet measures less than half an inch in diameter. So tiny. But in the memory of a once-young boy, that little thing still brings joy over sixty years later.

A PRAYER

Dear God, please remind me that no act is too small for you to grow it into big, lasting delight.

12

Be Brave

Be strong and courageous.
—Joshua 1:9

Being brave is not always easy, but it's almost always worth taking the deep breath to just do it—even if "it" is very small.

When I was thirteen, my family lived near a cornfield and thus had regular house visits from mice. I was always aware that they could show up in unexpected places, but one night when I pulled down my bedspread and saw a gray lump under my loosely woven blanket, I had a full-scale freakout.

"Ahhh, there's a mouse in my bed!" I—always a wimp when it came to dealing with small intruders— screamed to my mom as I ran into the kitchen. "Pleeease get him out of there!"

Well, that was a challenge. If she marched into my room and yanked the blanket off the bed, he'd just dash away. A mouse trap was out of the question. (What self-respecting rodent would take the bait of a trap shoved in his face?)

Finally, she bravely decided to take a hammer to his skull.

I cowered in the kitchen as Mom crept down the hallway to my room, hammer poised over her head. Then, *wham*! I heard her weapon hit the bed once . . . twice . . . and a third time.

Then, after a long silence, she emerged from my room empty-handed. Laughing.

Finally catching her breath, she told me, "When I lifted the blanket, I saw I'd just beaten the living daylights out of one of your hair curlers!"

Granted, when God asks you to act with courage, the issues and consequences are often bigger than this one. But He also may invite you to be brave in less dire straits—because, as Luke 16:10 reminds us, the little things also count. And if you can be brave in a small matter, you never know when it will result in a big splash of joy.

A PRAYER

Dear God, thank you for your ample supply of brave—no matter what I'm facing.

13

Pray Anyway

How much more will your Father in heaven
give good gifts to those who ask him!
—Matthew 7:11

The first time I remember praying was one hot July night when I was ten years old.

My father had been sick for about a week. It was upsetting to see him ill, so, full of childlike faith, I submitted a request to the Almighty: "Dear God, please make my daddy well."

Then I promptly went to sleep, confident in God's ability to take care of this.

On Wednesday the doctor said he seemed improved, so that night I prayed the same prayer.

On Thursday, my daddy died.

A nice lady at church told me that God did indeed answer my prayers—that my daddy was well. He was just well in heaven. I wanted to believe her, but it seemed like a mean joke for God to play on my family.

For a long time after that, whenever I'd ask God to keep my family safe, I'd PS my prayer with "*You* know what I mean." He had become to me the God of Trick Answers. "Why pray at all?" I wondered.

Still, I prayed anyway, and I discovered as the years passed that even when He didn't give me what I asked for, He always gave me something to get me through. Following the loss of my father, God gave me my older brother who picked up the baton as well as a sixteen-year-old boy could. He took my friends and me miniature golfing, trick-or-treating, and rock and rolling at our first concert. On my wedding day, he walked me down the aisle.

I will never stop thanking God for the gift of my brother.

Similar to me, the apostle Paul didn't get an answer to prayer that he wanted, but he got what he needed (2 Corinthians 12:9). That's how prayer can be, friend. God might grant your wishes or He might not. But if you pray anyway, He will always give you something—or someone—to get you through.

A PRAYER

Dear God, please help me find joy in knowing you've got me covered either way.

14

Hold Space

Carry each other's burdens.
—Galatians 6:2

When someone is in crisis, often our first response is to spring into action, and we're frustrated by our inability to make the pain go away despite our frantic efforts.

But sometimes the most helpful, soul-nourishing thing we can do is "hold space" for them—to simply sit with someone in their pain.

When my father died, I remember people immediately emerged with casseroles, fluffy Jell-O salads, cards, and flowers. It felt like one hundred EMTs rushing in, desperately tying tourniquets to try to stop the bleeding.

Which, of course, they couldn't.

The funeral was on a Saturday; the next day I asked to go to church. When people saw me and said, "I'm so surprised to see you here," I didn't understand it. Church was where I felt safe and surrounded. Why wouldn't I want to be there?

True, they couldn't fix my father's absence. But they were just there, and that was enough.

One day years later, when our mother was deep in dementia,

my brother simply sat with her on a couch in silence, holding her hand for an hour. He was just there, and that was enough.

Of course we want to stop the pain. But as Eugene Peterson advises, "Instead of continuing to focus on preventing suffering—which we simply won't be very successful at anyway—perhaps we should begin entering the suffering, participating insofar as we are able—entering the mystery and looking around for God."*

You might find him in a casserole. Or a fluffy Jell-O salad.

Or in your very own hand, holding someone else's when there's nothing else you can do.

A PRAYER

Dear God, when life is broken and behaving badly, I want so much to make my loved one's pain disappear. Please teach me how to give the gift of "holding space," and remind me that, for now, that just might be enough.

*Eugene Peterson, introduction to Job, *The Message: The Bible in Contemporary Language* (Colorado Springs: NavPress, 2002).

15

Celebrate a Memory

The Lord is close to the brokenhearted.
—Psalm 34:18

I had been a daddy's girl, no doubt about it.

After he died, I remember our first Christmas without him. (And aren't those firsts after loss always the worst?) I was staring out my bedroom window on Christmas Eve, watching the sky rain—no magical snow, no magical anything that year. We had relatives over for dinner, and my mom had made asparagus casserole. I hated asparagus casserole.

Everything was wrong, and as I watched the sky dump its gloom on our already sad lives, I imagined that God's tears were falling with our own.

Where is the joy in life when you feel that even God is crying with you?

Maybe it's tucked into a memory.

I began to think about all I missed about my daddy: his silly sense of humor, like when he'd throw his arm around my mom in our Rambler station wagon and belt out "Ridin' along in my automobile, my baby beside me at the wheel!"

Or the way he expressed appropriate amazement at my piano playing and baton twirling.

Or when we would take a very special trip every Saturday morning to "our" place, a beloved place that would nourish my heart for the rest of my life: the dump. Mountains of stinky stuff, but with a few treasures lodged somewhere in the rubble. You could find them if you kept a keen eye out and were diligent with your search.

Not unlike our lives.

Your sorrow may never disappear—but maybe you have a sweet memory to treasure in your grieving heart that will help you feel God's nearness and cause you to thank Him for someone special, whose life you can celebrate for the rest of your own life.

A PRAYER

Dear God, thank you for the gift of soul-filling memories. Please bring a few to mind when you and I are crying together.

16

Anticipate Joy

Keep your eyes open, hold tight to your
convictions, give it all you've got, be resolute.
—1 Corinthians 16:13 MSG

Ever see a five-year-old start crying before he even gets a shot? That was me before my first MRI. I am somewhat claustrophobic and was panicking about being trapped in a tube for half an hour.

On the day of the procedure, my heart pounding, I walked into the room and was greeted by a sweet technician who said these magic words: "Would you like to listen to some music?"

I requested a radio station to help me feel connected to the outside world, and I found the whole experience wasn't nearly as unpleasant as I'd feared. But I had spent days consumed with anxiety—days when I could have been doing something halfway fun.

Negative anticipation is powerful. You have felt it in your own life. But hear this: As powerful as negative anticipation is, living in anticipation of joy is even more potent.

What if we approached each day anticipating joy? What if we woke up every morning looking forward to a bit of cheer, even if life is going bananas?

What if, when our eyes first opened, we asked God to show us delight that day, and then lived in confidence He would do just that? After all, His Word encourages us to rejoice (2 Corinthians 13:11), so shouldn't we expect Him to lend a hand?

What if we followed the lead of an eight-year-old boy whose mom shared their conversation on Twitter. As she was buckling him into the back seat of their car, he asked, "Is it okay to throw the confetti in my pocket?"

"No, not in the car! Why do you have confetti in your pocket?"

"It's my emergency confetti. I carry it everywhere in case there is good news."*

A PRAYER

Dear God, please help me live every day anticipating joy, always ready with confetti in my pocket to celebrate the goodness you have waiting for me.

*Ana the Distracted Gardener, Twitter, November 22, 2020.

17

Enjoy the Age You Are

I praise you, for I am fearfully and wonderfully made.
Wonderful are your works; my soul knows it very well.

—Psalm 139:14 ESV

When my grandson graduated from preschool, his classmates had a parade, each child in a different decorated car. I loved watching him hang out the window, excitedly yelling at his friends. But on the drive home he was uncharacteristically quiet, so I asked him, "Hey, what's the matter, buddy?"

His reply: "I wanna be five forever."

I'm right there with you, pal.

The challenges of moving from one age to another start early, and as we travel to the next chapter, sometimes we think there's no going back. But writer Anne Lamott offers hope from a different perspective:

> I am all the ages I've ever been. You realize this at some point about your child—even when your kid is sixteen, you can see all the ages in him, the baby wrapped up like a burrito, the one-year-old about to walk, the four-year-old napping,

the ten-year-old on a trampoline. . . . Every age we've ever been is who we are.*

Indeed. And every age we've ever been can help us find joy in whatever age we are.

To do this, try remembering each stage of your life and what brought you delight. Then find a way to revisit the soul of that delight now. Of course, you may not be able to climb trees like you did when you were five, but you can spend time in the outdoors that made your heart sing then—and now, since the soul of that child is still in you, waiting for a chance to come out and play.

A PRAYER

Dear God, please teach me how to resurrect the heart of joy in all the mess I have ever been and will be.

---

*Anne Lamott, *Grace (Eventually): Thoughts on Faith* (New York: Riverhead, 2008), 78.

PART TWO

Young Adulthood

18

Let Music Take You to Joy

Shout for joy to the LORD, all the earth,
burst into jubilant song with music.

—Psalm 98:4

You probably know that the power of music is mighty and mysterious.

It can make your spirit blast off, move you to tears, take you back to a memory you thought you'd forgotten.

It can make you feel young or old, inspire longing, compel you to dance,

light a fire, set a mood, inspire romance,

help you grieve, remind you of someone you love,

toss you into a pit of despair, and usher you straight into the presence of God.

You're probably already thinking of songs that have done this in your own life.

Just remember: the music that's worked its way into your soul can also unwrap a joyful heart.

Every time I hear "Misty," I remember playing that song on the piano in our high school stage band. One evening we were setting up to perform for a dinner, and the only piano available was a large upright that had to be moved. Despite the sign that said, "DO NOT MOVE THIS PIANO," I gave it a big ol' shove.

Of course, the upright promptly became a downright, hitting the wall and somebody's trombone on the way to the floor. Everyone stopped eating and turned to look at the girl lying sideways on the fallen piano.

Later the venue manager asked our band director who the offender was, because he said, "Some *gorilla* must have pushed that thing over."

"Misty" is on my list of songs that make me laugh (for very unromantic reasons).

What does your heart need right now, friend? Would you consider asking God to help you create a playlist of songs that make your soul take flight above your circumstances?

A PRAYER

Dear God, thank you so much for your gift of music.
Would you show me what tunes would lead me to your joy?

19

Forgive Somebody

Be kind to one another, compassionate, forgiving each
other, just as God in Christ also has forgiven you.

—Ephesians 4:32 NASB

Somebody do you wrong?

Maybe a small misdeed has lodged itself in your mind for a while. It doesn't exactly make you or break you, but it might send you on an undesirable trajectory toward a strained relationship or dark thoughts.

I understand. A few words from my past festered comfortably in a corner of my mind for many years. But one day I decided it was time to say, "I forgive you, dear lady at the preschool my daughter attended, when you looked at my precious three-year-old and said, 'What a beautiful little girl!' And right after I thanked you, you studied my face and added, 'She must look like her daddy.'"

Nope.

I also forgive you, well-meaning person who set me up on a blind date with a guy who asked, "What does she look like?" And you replied, "Well, she's no Miss America, but she's a lot of fun."

Ouch.

So. Someone has lobbed a few zingers at you too.

A parent. A spouse. A child. A friend. Even a stranger.

There's a risk, of course, in extending forgiveness. We have to release some comfortable self-pity and be willing to let it go for the sake of our own mental health.

But "earth is forgiveness school," said Anne Lamott.* And it's entirely possible at any given time for us all to move up a grade.

Even if it means saying, "I forgive you, guy from my past, for saying, 'I don't know why I keep hanging around you. You're sure not the prettiest girl I've ever been out with.'"

Fortunately, one does not have to forget in order to forgive. We just have to be willing.

A PRAYER

Dear God, please give me your heart to offer grace to those who have hurt me, remembering that, along the way, you and others have forgiven me.

*Anne Lamott, "12 Truths I Learned from Life and Writing," TED2017, filmed in April 2017, YouTube, 9:59, https://www.ted.com/talks/anne_lamott_12_truths _i_learned_from_life_and_writing?subtitle=en.

20

Let the Door Close

God can do anything, you know—far more than you could
ever imagine or guess or request in your wildest dreams!
—Ephesians 3:20 MSG

When I was in college, I had no idea what I wanted to do with the rest of my life. I only knew that I required adequate amounts of fun and that I loved school.

Naturally, I decided to become an elementary school teacher.

In the classroom during my student teaching, however, I quickly learned that young children know a pushover when they see one. I might as well have walked into their space in a clown suit with a "Kick Me!" sign on my back.

Student teaching in middle school was no better.

On the first day there, my supervisor left me in charge of the room for a minute. In record time, the little rapscallions had locked me in the media closet.

In that sacred space, the Lord revealed to me that corralling and educating children was not the path to living my best life.

That (literal *and* figurative) closed door was discouraging, but eventually I realized I still loved school. A couple years later, God led me to a career I loved: teaching college students.

Friend, have you ever found yourself on the wrong side of a closed door, asking God, "What just happened?" Take heart.

Parker Palmer, in his book *Let Your Life Speak*, says that "each time a door closes, the rest of the world opens up. All we need to do is stop pounding on the door that just closed, turn around— which puts the door behind us—and welcome the largeness of life that now lies open to our souls."*

The Bible tells us that God not only has created us to do good works, but He has already prepared them for us, like gifts just waiting for us to discover them (1 Corinthians 2:10). But journeying toward the good things ahead of us means walking beyond what lies behind.

A PRAYER

Dear God, I pray that you would show me the possibilities ahead when I turn around and put that closed door behind me.

---

*Parker Palmer, *Let Your Life Speak: Listening for the Voice of Vocation* (San Francisco: Jossey-Bass, 1999), 54.

21

Use Your Words

Pleasant words are a honeycomb, sweet to
the soul and healing to the bones.

—Proverbs 16:24 NASB

Teacher Melanie McCabe found a way to turn the Valentine trauma she once experienced into a soul treat for her students.

In sixth grade, she told them, she was in love with a cute boy named David.

On party day, she dumped her cards on her desk and saw one huge, glittery card with the words "To a Queen of a Valentine" on top. Excited, she nearly fainted when she turned it over and saw his name.

Then she read the special message above the signature: "To the Ugliest Girl in Our Class."

Naturally, it ruined Valentine's Day for her and did considerable damage to her self-esteem.

But that hideous experience motivated her years later to throw her students a "party that celebrates kindness instead of cruelty." She provided construction paper and markers and instructed the kids to write something positive and sincere to every person in the class.

As she watched them read what people had written to them, the room came alive with joy.

After the party, some students kept their valentines and read them when they were feeling low. Parents emailed to tell her that the valentine exchange had boosted their child's confidence. And one class presented her with a valentine addressed, "To the Prettiest Girl in the Room." She still keeps that one hanging next to her desk.*

Affirming words have tremendous power to bring joy. Is there someone you know who needs some tangible on-paper reassurance of his or her value, not only to God but to you?

A PRAYER

Dear God, I would love it if you would allow me to be the catalyst to turn a day—and maybe even a life—around. Please show me someone who needs my words today.

*Melanie McCabe, "I Was Bullied on Valentine's Day As a Kid. Here's How I Spread Kindness As a Teacher Now," *Reader's Digest*, January 20, 2021, AOL, https://www.aol.com/lifestyle/bullied-valentine-day-kid-spread-161759541.html.

22

Be Bold

On the day I called, You answered me; You
made me bold with strength in my soul.

—Psalm 138:3 NASB

When I was in college, I had a crush on a boy who was my friend. My all-women's dorm was sponsoring a dance, so I decided to bite the bullet and ask him to be my date when we were talking one night.

Amused, he could tell I was nervous about something, and decided to make the most of my discomfort. He took a seat, put his feet up on the desk, folded his arms across his chest, and said, grinning, "Now . . . what was it you wanted to ask me?"

This irritating display of bravado from such a cocky boy made me determined to play it off, so I quickly collected my courage.

"Buddy, I'm about to give you the opportunity of a lifetime."

"And this is?"

"To take me to a dance."

Who could resist that invite? He said yes.

I just needed one more crucial piece of information, so I asked the question that, back then, women were *never* supposed to ask: "So how do you feel about me, anyway?"

I know. I can't believe I said that either. But I was *not* into wasting time playing games. I just wanted to know the ground rules so I could proceed with the most joy.

He looked at the floor in an aw-shucks way and said, "Well, I don't think a guy could ask for more in a girl."

All righty then. It was a date, and we could slow-dance un-awkwardly.

Friend, do you need to act with boldness? To move beyond the security of the "safe"? Granted, bold doesn't always work out well. But living courageously and true to who we are? Totally what God calls us to do.

A PRAYER

Dear God, being bold is not always my strength. Please help me rely on you to nudge me into courage.

23

Say "I Love You"

Now these three remain: faith, hope and
love. But the greatest of these is love.

—1 Corinthians 13:13

It's quite possibly the weirdest phrase in the English language. Because, oddly enough, it's a nonquestion that demands an answer: If someone says, "I love you," the hoped-for response is, of course, "I love you too."

But what if you put yourself out there in such a way, and get something else?

When my then-boyfriend Ben first said, "I love you," that phrase meant (to me) a big commitment.

And I was *not* ready for that gig. Personally, I was afraid—not of being vulnerable or being hurt but of growing up.

So in response to Ben's declaration of affection, I said . . . "I'm glad."

I know. So lame.

I eventually came around, but we all know how risky it is to offer your heart with those words in any relationship.

Maybe you are shy about doing so. But if you are privileged enough to have known the exquisite agony of loving someone for the long haul, yet you've never actually looked that person in the eyes and said, "I love you," would you consider doing it—even if it's hard for you?

Because your friend might be going through a rough time right now, and this reminder would be an incredible lift.

Maybe your mother hasn't heard it from you lately. Or ever. And telling her would reassure her that, even when she feels lonely, she's not alone.

Your brother might need to feel that someone is in his corner—for keeps.

Or maybe—especially if your relationship has been difficult lately—your child needs reassurance that you always have and always will keep the love coming. No matter what.

Such a simple, powerful phrase can lift up, inspire confidence, provide comfort in grief or failure, assure forgiveness, and even heal.

A PRAYER

Dear God, please give me the courage to say those three words out loud, not from pressure or obligation, but rather from . . . well, love.

24

Wallow

Blessed are those who mourn, for they will be comforted.
—Matthew 5:4

Sometimes, in the middle of circumstances we can't control, the quickest path to joy is to wallow in the mire for a while.

I know: you may have been taught the opposite—to plow ahead. Keep walkin'. Fake it till you make it. Do *something*.

At some point, maybe yes. But not quite yet.

First, it might help to name your emotions. (Frustration? Anger? Grief? Anxiety?)

Then? Just sit for a bit.

When Ben had to leave Purdue University in Indiana to start work in Virginia, our relationship status was uncertain. His last night at Purdue was awful. We said our goodbyes, not knowing if our bond could stand the test of time and distance.

Then I schlepped back to my dorm and did the only logical thing you do in a crisis: I made a beeline for the vending machines. They contained nothing except orange cupcakes. I hated orange cupcakes, so I plunked my money in and grabbed a package.

Then I went up to the lobby, ripped it open, called my mom and wailed, "What if he forgets about me? What if he finds someone else?"

My mom could have told me to get myself together, to stop drowning my sorrows in food that I hated. Instead, she said, "I know you're scared, but if it's really meant to be, you'll find a way to make it work. And whatever it is you're eating, enjoy."

Because my mom apparently knew that sometimes you just need a bit of time to wallow.

Are you suffering in circumstances beyond your control? Please remember that God did not create you to be a superhero who can withstand a hail of emotional bullets without pausing in your forward movement.

A PRAYER

Dear God, thank you for permission to plop down in my distress and wallow a little while as a first step toward joy.

25

Compromise

If it is possible, as far as it depends on
you, live at peace with everyone.
—Romans 12:18

Early in our marriage, Ben and I had our first big fight—I mean, enthusiastic disagreement—about doing the laundry.

As newlyweds, we had no washer or dryer. We were pretty much livin' on love, trying to save money any way we could. We didn't always see eye to eye, however, about how to do this.

We lived in the upstairs apartment of an old house, right across the road from his parents' home. I loved his parents, but I thought since we were now adults, we should prove that to them and ourselves.

So I took our clothes to the nearest laundromat. And every time I went, I could see dollar signs in Ben's eyes as he thought about all the quarters I was spending.

I shouldn't have been surprised, then, when he said, "You know, Mumma said we could use their washer and dryer. We could go over there, throw the clothes in, and she'd put them in the dryer."

This was a most generous offer, but I bristled, saying, "We are not teenagers! We need to do our own laundry!"

"But it's costing so much money we don't need to spend!" he would counter.

Back and forth we went until finally I said, "Okay, but if the laundry gets done at Mumma's, then *you* do the laundry."

Bingo. He was most happy with this arrangement, and as it turned out, so was I.

How about you? If you're locking horns with someone a little too often, it might help to remember that compromise is essentially grace. And although it's important to establish boundaries, and flexibility should never be a sacrifice of your personhood, sometimes when two sides give a little, you can meet in the middle—with joy.

A PRAYER

Dear God, I really like getting my way, as you know. Please show me when it's time to negotiate.

26

Hug

There is a time for everything, and a season for
every activity under the heavens . . . a time to
embrace and a time to refrain from embracing.

—Ecclesiastes 3:1, 5

Are you a hugger? Or maybe you're more inclined to shy away
from the big squeeze?

Soon after my husband and I were married, it became evident
to me that we had been born into differing family hug cultures.
My family was not stingy with affection, but I learned right away
that Ben's people hugged *all* the time—to say hello, goodbye, and
everything in between.

Mind you, I loved these folks right from the start, and I totally
understood being glad to see people you love after being apart.
There's nothing like exuberant, celebrative reunions, and expres-
sions of gladness after separation are natural and right.

But I had a hard time believing anybody could be *that* glad to
see me, because wow . . . we lived across the street, people. We
saw them every day.

So if you are not prone to excessive hugging, I get it.

But when our nation was mired in a global pandemic, and you
and I were, for safety's sake, limited in whom we could hug, our

health may have suffered in other ways—because the emotional and physical benefits of hugging are many.

A hug may make an individual feel joyful by reducing feelings of loneliness and the harmful physical effects of stress. Hugs can also change negative moods by boosting hormones like dopamine, serotonin, and oxytocin.

Maybe doctors should start writing more prescriptions for this stuff, since God hardwired us to benefit from hugging. It costs nothing but a little time—and maybe a little space.

And one dose could be the remedy for someone's joyless day.

A PRAYER

Dear God, please help me recognize when someone in my orbit needs to be in the circle of at least one of my arms.

27

Adapt

Be kind and compassionate to one another.
—Ephesians 4:32

I grew up in the Midwest, but after Ben and I were married, we settled in his home state of Virginia, which was a bit of a culture shock for me. However, I was eager to experience the joy of adapting to the language and customs of his people in this strange land.

One day I decided to cook some navy beans and ham, and had been told by a few seasoned Southerners that it was best to throw a ham hock in the pot.

Great. All I had to do was figure out what that was.

The butcher at the grocery store explained that it was a pork knuckle, which was bad enough, but I was truly horrified when I took it out of the package at home and saw that this appendage of swine actually had *hair* on it.

I wondered if it was defective merchandise that had somehow escaped quality control at the pig leg factory. I was, however, too embarrassed to take it back to the store, so I did the only thing I knew to do: adapt.

That afternoon when Ben came home, he found me intent

on my task. "What in the world are you doing with the pig's ankle?" he asked.

"Tweezing it," I said, as though I did this every day when he went to work. "You don't want hair in your food, do you?"

I now know there are other ways of dealing with the issue.

But that evening I proudly served up the product of my adaptive skills: a perfectly lovely dinner of beans and hairless ham.

Sometimes joy is a product of adjustment, my friend.

A PRAYER

Dear God, please keep me flexible in mind and heart toward others so we can all share the delight you are so anxious to give us.

28

Ask for God's Perspective

Do not be afraid; do not be discouraged, for the LORD
your God will be with you wherever you go.

—Joshua 1:9

Camping to some folks means spending the night at a mom-and-pop motel instead of the Ritz Carlton.

To others, however, camping is hauling your supplies on your back over rough terrain, inflating a raft to get you across a river, deflating the raft once you've crossed the river, hiking until it gets dark, then throwing your sleeping bag on the grass and settling in for an unsettling slumber. Or no slumber, since there is no tent, not even a few inches of nylon between you and whatever is lurking around in the middle of the night.

That was my husband and me camping with his cousins in Wyoming.

I, for one, found the whole scenario very disturbing as darkness fell and a whole creepy chorus of unfamiliar thumpings and howlings surrounded us.

"Ah, don't worry," said one of the guys, an experienced

outdoorsman familiar with the area. "You'll be fine out here. It's as safe as being in God's hip pocket."

Well, that was reassuring until my fears got the best of me and I wondered, "What if God decides to sit down?"

Have you ever wondered the same—that the truly undesirable might happen in an unknown future over which you have no control?

Of course. We all have.

But, friend, God has control. David the psalmist-king, who knew all about fearful circumstances, wrote, "In peace I will lie down and sleep, for you alone, LORD, make me dwell in safety" (Psalm 4:8). So it may help to ask for God's perspective on whatever you're facing and fearing.

That night in the wild, He told me, "I've given you Mountain Men who know what those noises are and have excellent night vision. They are surrounding you in the dark—and so am I."

A PRAYER

Dear God, thank you for guiding my thoughts about my fears and helping me feel safe in your "hip pocket." Remind me that you neither slumber nor sleep. Nor sit down.

29

Lift Someone Up

Therefore encourage one another and build each other up.
—1 Thessalonians 5:11

Our struggle with infertility was taking my husband and me on a long, heavy-hearted journey—month after month of endless doctors' visits, lots of poking and prodding, reports of "there's nothing more we can do," and prayers not answered the way we thought God should respond.

One year, I desperately wanted to give Ben a birthday present that would bring him (and me) some joy despite our frustration and sorrow.

So I decided to send myself to him.

I found a box large enough to hold my entire body, wrapped the box up like a big birthday present, and arranged for Lloyd, a maintenance man in Ben's office building, to meet me in the basement and help hoist me into the box, which was on a dolly. Then into the elevator we rolled and headed up to the lobby, where we met a gentleman from a singing telegram service I had enlisted to deliver the surprise.

The telegram man took over and pushed me into Ben's office, yelling his name and singing "Happy Birthday." As Ben took the lid off the box, I jumped out and watched his face register first shock and then delight as he and everyone else in the room burst into laughter.

What started out as a crazy birthday present ended up offering some levity to our sagging spirits—not only for the moment but every time we recalled the memory.

Even if jumping out of a big box in front of a bunch of people is something you are unwilling to do this side of heaven (and maybe on the other side too), please know there's no limit to the creative, sometimes unorthodox, ways you can encourage others.

A PRAYER

Dear God, please give me the eyes—and the heart, even when mine is breaking—to see how I can lift someone else up to joy.

30

Walk in the Rain

This is the day the LORD has made. We
will rejoice and be glad in it.
—Psalm 118:24 NLT

One rainy day when my daughter was four years old, I had a lot to do and was cleaning the house when she approached me with this perfectly ridiculous suggestion: "Mommy," she said, "let's put on our swimsuits and get umbrellas and go walking in the rain."

To be clear: my first thought was, "This is wrong on so many levels."

For one thing, we lived in a neighborhood where the houses were close together; we all knew everybody's business. So, for sure, everyone would be able to see Jamie and me in our beachwear, ambling down the street like we did this all the time. I feared turning into a side show for the neighborhood circus.

And, come on, it was so *rainy*. And I was so *busy*.

I almost said no.

But when she looked at me with those excited, big blue eyes, I thought, Oh well. She's only four once.

So we did it. We both put on our swimsuits, grabbed our umbrellas, and went for a twenty-minute walk in the rain.

Thirty-nine years later, she remembers those twenty minutes. So do I.

And that priceless memory is always God's gentle reminder that He made this day and provided all the opportunities for joy in it—no matter how small, no matter how goofy-looking—and that I should embrace them for all they're worth. Which is quite a lot.

A PRAYER

Dear God, how many invitations to joy have I turned down because I was too busy, or didn't want to look silly, or some other such nonsense? Please wake me up to the wonder in each day, and nudge me to say "Yes!" when you say, "Let's go walk in the rain."

31

Be Somebody's Huckleberry

A friend loves at all times, and a brother
is born for a time of adversity.

—Proverbs 17:17

The phrase "I'm your huckleberry," which became popular in the 1800s, used to mean "I'm the man for the job." Then it was made famous in modern times in the 1993 movie *Tombstone* when Doc Holliday said to Johnny Ringo, "I'm your huckleberry. That's just my game."

More recently and widely, though, the phrase has come to indicate "I am your partner; I will stick with you; I will be on your side." That is the kind of huckleberry we all love—a faithful and involved friend who helps ease life's load when it gets heavy (Galatians 6:2).

Every joyful life has at least one of these; every joyful life needs to *be* one of these.

And what does being a huckleberry look like? Maybe this:

My friend Bart was training for a half marathon in Virginia

when his running partner backed out. So he had to plan to run the race by himself.

Patrick, his good friend, who ran all the time and was in great shape, called to encourage Bart, saying, "Just know that on that day, I'll be running too and thinking about you."

Months went by. Then on the night before the race, a surprise showed up at Bart's door: It was Patrick, saying, "I told you I'd be running too . . . right next to you."

The following day they ran the race, Patrick at Bart's slower pace the whole time. Halfway through, Bart started experiencing pain. Patrick asked him, "What hurts the most?"

Bart answered, "My left knee. What's hurting you the most?"

Patrick's response: "Your left knee."

That right there is some huckleberry.

Who is your huckleberry, friend? And even more important: Who needs *you* to be a huckleberry—

a willing adventurer,

an advocate,

a sounding board,

a safe space,

a soft place,

a mischief maker,

a burden taker,

a comfort giver?

A PRAYER

Dear God, thanks so much for good friends. Help me, please, to know when someone needs me to ride—or run—alongside them.

32

Let Your Heart Break Again

Do not forget to do good and to share with others,
for with such sacrifices God is pleased.

—Hebrews 13:16

Misery = no fun ever.

But maybe you can use your misery to help someone with theirs.

A while back in Boston, my daughter, Jamie, had two extensive surgeries. The procedure involved breaking her poor dysplastic hips, repositioning the bones, wiring them back together, and sending her off on crutches for four months each time.

It was, she would tell you, the essence of misery.

But right in the middle of the worst of it, Jamie announced that once she recovered, she wanted to come back and volunteer at the hospital.

"I don't care what I'd be doing," she said. "I'd scrub floors with a toothbrush if they needed me to." Which proves she was under the influence of God above, friends, because as I recall, she never scrubbed anything with a toothbrush but her teeth when she was living at home.

Eventually she did indeed return to the hospital to tend to children in the outpatient waiting room.

"It makes no sense," I thought, "going back to the place of your pain after you've healed."

Or does it?

What if your revisitation could help someone mend?

Could you venture out and encourage someone through

a divorce?

the loss of someone dear?

an illness?

long days of caregiving?

a dark night of the soul?

When the "this too shall pass" in your own life actually does pass, would you be willing to risk coming back to your own pain to travel with another soul through theirs?

It could possibly involve a few tears or some of your time or emotional energy.

But it's all holy ground—the oh-so-comforting place where "I know how you feel" is true, not trite.

A PRAYER

Dear God, please help me be willing to let my own heart break again to help someone else's mend.

33

Figure It Out

If any of you lacks wisdom, you should ask God.

—James 1:5

There's joy in using that God-given brain of yours to figure a few things out.

When my friends Bob and Nancy took a trip to Yosemite with their three children one summer, they packed for the warm June temperatures they had left in Virginia.

They learned in short order, however, that this was a big mistake.

Lying in their tent in subfreezing temperatures one night, in dire need of warm clothing they didn't have, they tried to think of a way to stay warm short of exiting the park in an act of utter defeat.

What to do?

They knew that you lose a lot of heat from your head, but they had no hats, because who from Virginia thinks about needing hats in the summer? Eventually, however, with a little brain power and ingenuity, they found a joyful way to stay relatively warm and have a good laugh at the same time.

Well, the parents had a good laugh, anyway. The children said they'd be mortified if anyone ever found out they had all spent the night with their underwear on their heads.

(It was a long time ago. All is forgiven.)

There's probably a challenge in your life right now that needs some problem-solving skills. It might involve

a relationship,

a life change,

a move,

a health issue,

finances,

care needs for loved ones,

or so much more.

Whatever you're encountering these days—from the smallest tasks to life-altering issues—maybe you could ask God to help you dig into resourcefulness you may not even know you have.

A PRAYER

Dear God, I've got this problem that needs solving. Please open my mind to the possibilities beyond my limited gaze.

PART THREE

Midlife

34

Give a Boomerang Gift

Those who refresh others will themselves be refreshed.
—Proverbs 11:25 NLT

There's no joy quite like the kind that comes from giving a gift you know someone will love.

My friend Sue was about to turn fifty, and I wanted to give her something special.

One day I remembered the time she told me that someday she wanted a ride on a Harley.

So I found John, a Harley guy at our church who said he'd be delighted to assist in making her dream come true. Sue and her husband would be spending the weekend with us, so about five minutes before John was to show up, I said, "Sue, I have a birthday surprise for you!"

I cued up "Born to Be Wild" on the house speakers. When the doorbell rang, I dragged her to the door, and opened it with a flourish.

And there stood John, smiling, all dressed to ride, with a spare helmet in his hand.

"My friend, behold your birthday present!" I fairly shouted at Sue—but to my surprise, the look on her face was not one of joy. More like terror.

She thought I was giving her a *man* for her birthday.

"No, no! He's going to give you a ride on that," I said, as I pointed to the bike in the street.

And honestly, no one has ever been so ecstatic about a gift as *both* of us.

I helped her into a genuine black pleather jacket, then delighted in the sight of her on that motorcycle with outstretched arms, yelling, "Woo-hooooooo!" as they roared down the street in a cloud of dust and adventure.

Do you have a friend who could use a spot of joy today? With a little creativity, you could bring some levity to someone else and watch that joy boomerang to your own heart!

A PRAYER

Dear God, thank you for the joy that comes back to me when I give it to someone else!

35

Give a Compliment

Let everything you say be good and helpful, so that your
words will be an encouragement to those who hear them.

—Ephesians 4:29 NLT

One day in the Fort Lauderdale airport, while sitting on a bench
facing some automatic doors that opened to the outside, I
noticed that everybody who came through those doors was smiling. I knew there had to be something afoot because so many
random people in the same place are not grinning for no reason.
So I walked over and instantly found out the source of all that joy.

Every time someone strolled through those automatic doors, a
deep voice purred some kind of compliment, like "You're beautiful!" or a woman's voice would chirp, "Hi there! Good to see you.
Give me a big smile!"

It was brilliant, and it made me laugh out loud. "Who," I
wondered, "was sitting around one day, bored, and thought,
Hey, people need cheering up around here. Let's give them a few
compliments and see what happens."

Obviously, joy happens, judging from those smiles.

I wanted some of that.

So even though I had no reason to go outside, I walked through
that breezeway and heard, "Hi there! It's a beautiful day! I like

your shoes!" which made me laugh because I was wearing really crummy shoes. Obviously this voice was not attached to a set of eyes. Even so—what a joy!

If those words from fake people were so therapeutic, then surely, I thought, a real compliment from a real person with a real face would be even more uplifting.

And I was not wrong.

Who needs a boost from you today? Often we don't verbalize our uplifting thoughts toward others, but voicing a simple sincere compliment can feed someone's soul.

A PRAYER

Dear God, please make me aware of someone in my path who could use a little encouragement, and nudge me to give them a few uplifting words. From a real human.

36

Ask, "What's It Like to Be You?"

Clothe yourselves with compassion, kindness,
humility, gentleness and patience.

—Colossians 3:12

Do people ever exasperate you?

Of course they do.

When I first started teaching freshman English at Virginia Commonwealth University, I had no patience with students' chronic absence and inattentiveness. But after a few years, in an effort to understand their behavior, I began to ask them, "What's it like to be you?"

And I quickly discovered what was competing with whatever I was trying to teach.

She just found out she's pregnant and must decide what to do.

She was raped when she was twelve, and an assignment I made brought back too many memories.

He is a father of two, who just found out his wife is expecting twins and whose oldest son has leukemia.

She comes to class having worked all night in the ER.

She just found out over the phone that her mother has breast cancer.

Her little sister has run away again. Her mom called, begging her to come home and help find her.

His grandmother was an alcoholic. His father is an alcoholic. He got drunk last night and is terrified he's following in their footsteps.

They were all in my classes over the years, and knowing their stories helped me to be more compassionate and to work with them rather take their behavior personally.

Of course, there was that one time that I noticed a student distracted by something in the direction of my head. When I asked him what was on his mind, he said, "I have a question, Ms. Baughan. Do you do that to your hair on purpose?"

Sigh.

A PRAYER

Dear God, when people exasperate me, remind me that they too are living complicated, messy lives. Please gift me with patience and compassion.

37

Honor Your Body

Do you not know that your bodies are temples of the
Holy Spirit, who is in you, whom you have received
from God? You are not your own; you were bought at
a price. Therefore honor God with your bodies.

—1 Corinthians 6:19–20

Can we talk about what you look like?

My guess is, you're already cringing, which is sad because sometimes our perception of our own looks can keep us from a life of joy. And may I just say, "Ain't nobody got time for that."

If you're a regular person, there's probably something about your appearance that isn't okay with you, that you wish were different.

And if you have a few years of living behind you, you can't help but compare the you of today with the you of a couple decades ago. Or maybe there's something about you that's not like (your perception of) "everybody else." Maybe you have a lazy eye, or thinning hair, or a wonky gait, or crooked feet, or some extra fluff, or any one of countless possible bodily irregularities.

Of course, these days, rampant photoshopping and filtering don't help any normal person's self-esteem. Our body blues can lead us to some strange and destructive places.

That's most unfortunate.

Because though it's heartening to know that the God of the universe knows you by your beautiful soul, it might also help to remember that even the imperfect body surrounding that soul is giving you life.

Maybe part of honoring your body is a gentle acceptance of what is—and then an even slightly joyful focus on the limitless possibilities of what God can do through this come-as-you-are body.

A PRAYER

Dear God, I'm often frustrated with my physical body, but I pray you will keep reminding me it is a holy creation that surrounds my heart for you.

38

Sit in a Creek

I will refresh the weary and satisfy the faint.
—Jeremiah 31:25

Eleven days after September 11, 2001, Ben and I hiked to the bottom of the Grand Canyon.

Like everyone else's nerves, ours were on high alert, but our hiking group was still scheduled to make the trip. So, armed with the essentials (water and gorp, a trail mix made of peanuts, raisins, and never enough M&Ms), we made the descent and were greeted at the bottom by a thermometer that read 108 degrees.

I felt like throwing up.

In this sickening heat, though, we made a magnificent discovery: Bright Angel Creek. As we crossed the creek to get to camp, the most delicious feeling came over me as I stuck a hot foot into that cool, rushing water: I wanted very much just to sit down right in the middle of it, even though I had my hiking clothes on.

So I did.

And there, with my agitated heart and weary body, I talked to God about everything on my mind, especially evil and my terror of terrorists. But after a while, my focus shifted—to an electric blue sky and the sun setting the canyon on fire in shades of red and gold. And I had to thank Him for so much beauty, which was, I just knew, a taste of heaven.

An hour later I emerged from the water refreshed from the inside out.

And even though nothing in the world (or my world) had changed, God had given me the gift of re-creation—the same gift He offers all of us so often, and which we so often decline.

Don't pass yours up. Watch for those refreshing creek-soaking moments every day. And when you encounter one, go ahead— have a seat.

A PRAYER

Dear God, please show me what "sitting in the creek" would look like for me today: five minutes of prayer? Music? Silence? Dancing? And then help me take the time to let you adjust my perspective. Maybe with a little gorp. And extra M&Ms if possible.

39

Sample a Friend's Joy

A sweet friendship refreshes the soul.
—Proverbs 27:9 MSG

Sometimes you can up your joy quotient by venturing into the uncharted territory of a friend's good time. What better way to "rejoice with those who rejoice" (Romans 12:15) than tasting a slice of something in a loved one's world that gives that person joy?

I've never completely understood football, but my husband is a huge fan of the game, especially when his alma mater, Virginia Tech, is playing. One year, Tech was offering a football clinic for unenlightened souls like me whose basic knowledge starts and stops at "First and ten! Do it again!"

It sounded intriguing, so I signed up for what I thought would be a Football for Dummies day.

Alas, I could tell right away that this session was for people who already knew the game. We were inundated with sport-specific terms like "push the pocket," "stick and rip," and "outside hand knockdown skate rush." Then the instructors went on and on about tight ends, back ends, side ends, and split ends, or something like that. Not sure now.

I finished the class with quite a few unanswered questions, but it was fun anyway, being immersed in my best friend's favorite sport—especially at the close of the day when we were allowed to tour the football field. What a thrill to gaze up into the stands from down on the turf.

Then I had a brilliant idea: Why not end the experience by running the entire length of the field, raising my hands, nodding to the roar of the imaginary crowd?

So I did.

It was glorious. And twice the fun for having stepped into the gladness of someone special.

A PRAYER

Dear God, thank you for the opportunity to be refreshed by the enthusiastic heart of a friend, even if their taste in joy is different from mine. And show us, please, how to delight in a day well played.

40

Ask, "What If?"

Now to him who is able to do far more abundantly than
all that we ask or think, according to the power at work
within us, to him be glory in the church and in Christ
Jesus throughout all generations, forever and ever. Amen.

—Ephesians 3:20–21 ESV

Asking "What if?" can change the world.

For instance, how much less marvelous would the world be had someone not asked,

"What if we could land a human being on the moon?"

"What if there were a medicine that could eradicate polio?"

"What if we had phones that let us see each other while we were talking?"

I myself once thought, "What if I asked this boy to a dance?" We ended up married.

What if philanthropist Bob Goff hadn't asked a big "what if" after he was denied acceptance to law school? He told the dean he needed to become a lawyer in order to make a difference in the world.

The dean turned him down, but Bob apparently asked himself,

"What if I sat on a bench outside the dean's office, saying, 'You have the power to let me in. All you have to do is say, "Go buy your books."'"*

After two weeks, the dean relented. Goff then went on to defend victims of sex trafficking, bring food to remote African villages, and inspire millions of people to live adventurous lives.

Bob Goff's "what ifs" really have changed the world.

So what about you? Could you write down a "what if?" God may have put something on your heart that would propel your own story—and as a result, the stories of others—toward more meaning. More joy.

A PRAYER

Dear God, what if I could partner with you and your limitless possibilities to change my world . . . and the world? Let's go!

*Bob Goff, *Love Does: Discover a Secretly Incredible Life in an Ordinary World* (Nashville: Thomas Nelson, 2012); Marci Seither, "Bob Goff's Audacious Parenting Adventure," *Focus on the Family Magazine*, November 1, 2017, https://www.focusonthefamily.com/parenting/bob-goffs-audacious-parenting-adventure.

41

Celebrate Each Other

Love one another with brotherly affection.
—Romans 12:10 ESV

At some point in your life, you might need a little help in entertaining a group of people for the better part of an evening.

Often, it's true, when people come together, the presence of free food is enough to keep everyone quite happy. And time to talk is essential, for sure.

Not every gathering, however, is without stress. Sometimes the conversation doesn't flow. Maybe people are tired or tense. Maybe they're so familiar with each other that there's nothing new to say. Or maybe they don't know each other at all, and the chemistry isn't cookin'.

Whatever the reason, if you're looking for a little more joy in a gathering these days, here's an idea that will help you celebrate everyone in your space:

Just give each person (ten to fifteen people, more or less) an index card, and ask them to write down something about themselves that nobody else in the room knows. It can be about their dreams for the future, a talent they have, a weird habit they practice, something they love or hate, some crazy concept they believed as a child—anything, really.

Once everyone has finished writing, collect the cards and give them to a leader to read out loud. Then the group tries to guess who owns the information on each card.

Note: Always ask for a detailed explanation. That ensures you'll end up with an evening full of fabulous stories and with a heart that's a little bigger and more appreciative of those in your space.

Also note: This is a great activity to pull out of your hat if you're with a small group of people who are stuck in an elevator or at an airport waiting for a delayed flight—anywhere folks tend to get bored and cranky.

A PRAYER

Dear God, thanks so much for a way to connect with the people around me! Please help us celebrate each other the way you do.

42

Look for What's Left Behind

Always giving thanks to God the Father for
everything, in the name of our Lord Jesus Christ.
—Ephesians 5:20

Cleaning up is highly overrated.

Not that you want to be a slob, mind you, but leaving a mess sitting around for a while can increase the shelf life of your joy.

I figured this out one day when I saw two pairs of wet shoes drying out on our front porch swing. Smelly and ratty looking, they were definitely not adding any aesthetic value to our property. I told myself that I should move those things to the back of the house, where they wouldn't offend visitors.

But then I thought, "I don't want to move them." They reminded me of a great time we'd had that weekend on a rafting trip. They reminded me of laughter mixed with adrenaline and people I love.

So I left them there. For two weeks.

Not because I was too lazy to move them but because every

time I came home and unlocked the front door, I'd glance to the left, see that nasty footwear, and smile.

So here's a thought: It's okay to admire a perfectly set table. But how about taking a moment to enjoy the chaos on the table *after* a great dinner? Or a birthday cake *after* you've cut into it? Or wet towels hanging on the porch after a day of swimming? Or, like my Grandma Ellis, how about leaving the fingerprints of children on your windows for a few days?

It's tempting, I know, to want to clean up and get on to your next task. But the exquisite confections of this life are way too fleeting, and enjoying what's left behind just might extend the celebration into all of your days.

A PRAYER

Dear God, thank you for the imperfect afterglow of good times. Please help me pause to smile and be grateful.

43

Make Joy the Whole Game

God deals out joy in the present, the now.
—Ecclesiastes 5:19 MSG

One January, I was pretending to be interested in watching the Super Bowl when one of the ads made me literally sit up and take notice.

"What if we were wrong this whole time?" it asked. "Wrong in thinking that joy happens only at the end? After the sacrifice? After the commitment? After the win?"*

It was the only moment during the whole evening when I actually cheered with sincerity.

"What if joy is the whole game—not just the end game?"

Oh, the brilliance. We just might miss a lot of wonder if we focus all our joy only on the outcome.

A while back, my husband and several friends went golfing, all knowing that none of them were any good.

Actually, that's being kind. They were all perfectly awful—so

---

*"'Happy' Superbowl," YouTube, January 27, 2021, https://www.youtube.com /watch?v=eppEgrmFacQ.

awful that they let everyone who came up behind them play through. They spent the afternoon randomly whacking and retrieving balls from every sand trap on the golf course as they lurched around, doubled over, making fun of each other.

They ended up with a combined score of 680. Yes, 680 for four people.

But they walked through the door at the end of the day with their faces hurting from laughing so much. And Ben said he'd never had so much fun playing golf.

As always, there's more than one way to look at the win.

Friend, what does your "whole game" look like? The journey to vacation? To retirement? To healing? Whatever it is, invest your joy in *all* of it. Because when we are only preoccupied with results, we miss out on the gifts God may be offering us along the way.

There's a lot to be said for embracing the joy of the whole game.

A PRAYER

Dear God, make me aware of what I'm missing when I find my only fulfillment in success at the end of any of my endeavors.

44

Laugh at Yourself

A cheerful heart is good medicine.
—Proverbs 17:22

If you are old enough, you may remember a particular phenomenon in the 1990s called Glamour Shots. This business convinced people—mostly women—to stop in, get their hair teased and fluffed, have stage makeup applied, and choose a fancy outfit the likes of which would never be found in any regular person's closet.

All this, of course, for a photograph that supposedly could make even the plainest customer look like a movie star.

I thought it would be a nice Christmas present for my husband, so I made an appointment and showed up in the magic chair. And all went well until I sat in front of the camera. You see, my left eye tends to shut before my right eye, rendering most photos of me unacceptable by any standards. Even low ones.

After the shoot, as I was viewing the proofs on a computer screen, I felt someone behind me also looking at them. It was the manager.

"You don't have much to choose from there, do you?" he said.

Yes, they were that bad—so bad that he offered me another free session right then and there.

And finally, after *four hours* of being pouffed, costumed, and posed, I walked out of the place with photos of me with both eyes pretty much open.

Was it worth the time and money? Absolutely, if you measure value in the times I and plenty of other people have enjoyed laughing at those photos. One of them sits on my dresser even now and makes me smile every single morning.

Sometimes joy can come from a willingness to laugh at your own self as you bumble around this ol' serious life.

A PRAYER

Dear God, I pray that you would help me not to take myself too seriously all the time. Please show me how my laughter at my own foibles can brighten someone else's day.

45

Cry

Jesus wept.
—John 11:35

Ever feel like crying, but instead you made a heroic effort to stifle your tears?

You may have been overcome with the urge to unleash the waterworks for a variety of reasons.

Maybe you were feeling sentimental, frustrated, angry, grief stricken, or even happy. The reason you feel that urge doesn't seem to matter. You probably resist it. But why?

Sometimes, you don't want people to see you out of control. You might perform tricks like swallowing hard or breathing deeply to keep your emotions and your face in check.

Or maybe you just cry uncle and go for it, since it was probably going to happen anyway. And you learn once again that you cannot control the universe, even the tiny one inside you.

Sometimes you just don't want to look unattractive as you fall victim to the infamous ugly cry.

Or you don't want to appear soft, since some people see crying as a sign of weakness (which it is not).

Or you feel it might make people around you uncomfortable.

(I've heard several men say, "I just don't know what to do with a crying woman.")

But here's the good news: Crying can actually be beneficial. Tears have been found to flush stress hormones and other toxins out of your system and release endorphins to make you feel better. Tears can also give you a physical boost and reduce inflammation by releasing stored-up emotions and energy.

Obviously, as with hugging, God has wired our bodies with a host of natural remedies for our maladies. Sometimes we just don't take advantage of them. But we should—not just because it's healthy for us to release our tears but because they matter to God. "You have collected all my tears in your bottle," says Psalm 56:8 (NLT). "You have recorded each one in your book."

So be unashamed of your tears, my friend, and as you let it go, may you remember you're in the greatest of company.

Because even Jesus wept.

A PRAYER

Dear God, thank you for giving me the gift of tears and permission to cry unashamedly when I feel like it.

46

Embrace Tacky

Serve one another through love.

—Galatians 5:13 NASB

You probably have standards for a few areas in your life. Would you consider lowering those standards when it comes to opening up your home to friends?

One of the most fun gatherings I've ever hosted was a Tacky Party—the least stressful way to entertain, since every part of the evening was necessarily unimpressive and, of course, tacky.

I asked guests to bring food, just any old edible thing: potted meat, aerosol cheese product . . . whatever required zero effort.

And the guests were into it from the get-go. They wore anything from pajamas to leisure suits. They brought their zero-effort foods. Some came super early, some came late, some brought their uninvited kids, all just to be tacky.

And it totally didn't matter. There were no social gaffes because the whole event was pretty much a social gaffe.

Of course there was no formal entertainment, only tacky games that required guests to engage in undignified activities like yelling, hiding in closets, and contorting themselves into impossible positions.

Maybe a Tacky Party seems to you like a heinous way to spend an evening with friends, but you have the option of adapting it to make sure you can entertain in a way that stresses you not and delights everyone a lot.

Author Shauna Niequist has said that "true hospitality is when someone leaves your home feeling better about themselves, not better about you."*

Honoring your own uniqueness here will guarantee that your delight will energize and bless your guests long after they say good night.

A PRAYER

Dear God, thank you for giving me permission to lower my entertainment standards just to the point of joy.

---

*Shauna Niequist, keynote video, 2014 keynote videos—Allume, filmed October 29, 2014, X.com, https://x.com/sniequist/status/527468643794554880?lang=en. For excellent insights on hospitality, I recommend Shauna's best-selling book *Bread and Wine: A Love Letter to Life around the Table with Recipes* (Grand Rapids: Zondervan, 2020).

47

Act like a Kid

It is absolutely clear that God has called you to a free life.
—Galatians 5:13 MSG

Our pastor and his wife had an annual open house at their home every Christmas. One year I decided to wear a festive red suit with holly-printed tights. I felt so fancy.

Shortly after we arrived, I glanced out the window to see a gaggle of kids in the backyard, clustered around a giant vine—the kind that could support you if you took a notion to hop on, swing across a ditch, and hop off on the other side.

Of course, that's exactly what they were doing, and I watched them with longing, thinking about how I would like to join them. But I was an adult, a dressed-up adult to boot, and I saw no other grown people out there acting like chimpanzees.

Finally, though, I gave in to my juvenile instincts, walked outside, and asked to play. The kids were only too happy to give me a turn, so I jumped onto the vine and, with my best Tarzan yodel, swung across the ditch, landed on the other side, and unobtrusively slipped back into the house.

Honestly, those few glorious seconds of freedom put my grown-up life in perspective.

I did learn later that people had been staring out the window, wondering who that was, whooping around. "Oh," explained someone, "it's only Jill." Like that explained everything. Which it pretty much did.

Are you weary of "adulting" these days? Maybe you could inject a little joy into your grown-up responsibilities by acting like a child. After all, it's children—and children at heart—whom Jesus welcomes with open arms into His kingdom (Matthew 19:13–14).

Watch kids for a while and do what they do. Splash in a puddle, put on a superhero cape, go to a playground. Or jump on vines when they swing in your direction.

A PRAYER

Dear God, thank you for reminding me how therapeutic child's play can be. Alert me to every opportunity, please, even if I'm in my fancy clothes.

48

Tell Your Story

May the God of hope fill you with all joy and
peace as you trust in him, so that you may overflow
with hope by the power of the Holy Spirit.

—Romans 15:13

After a mastectomy, Dawn Barton went shopping for a prosthetic breast. When she found just the right one, she named it Lucky.

During what she calls the Summer of Lucky, her family enjoyed several days of boating. At one point, she decided to jump off the side of the boat in an exuberant display of freedom; however, the moment she hit the water, she felt Lucky escape from her swimsuit.

I can't lose Lucky! she thought, in a panic.

Then suddenly, about fifteen feet away, Lucky burst out of the sea like a torpedo. Previously Dawn wasn't even aware that Lucky could float.

Everyone on the boat laughed so hard they couldn't speak. Or breathe, even.

Dawn has told this story repeatedly to give others a measure of gladness in the middle of hardship. "Because in times like these," she says, "each little win is worth replaying over and over again."*

*Dawn Barton, *Laughing through the Ugly Cry: And Finding Unstoppable Joy* (Nashville: Thomas Nelson, 2020), 59.

Thousands of people have been heartened by Dawn's story about how God has helped her through other struggles in her life too—not only breast cancer but also her divorce, the death of her infant daughter, and her rape.

You should tell your story too.

Oh, you may think your own story is not important or exciting enough. But consider those you might inspire by sharing your struggles and triumphs, your failures and victories, your story of coming to faith and losing your faith and then getting it back again in a whole new wrapper . . . and more.

A PRAYER

Dear God, thank you for helping me through the worst of times. Please let me know when I can encourage someone else with stories from my life.

49

Go for It

I have come that they may have life, and have it to the full.
—John 10:10

Sometimes joy lands in your lap; other times, you might have to pursue it.

Such was the case when my mom and I were at the Virginia State Fair, passing a photo stand where you could get your picture taken with a chimpanzee.

"Mom, let's get our picture taken with the chimp!" I pleaded.

I was thirty-five years old at the time and still begging my seventy-year-old mom to let me do fun stuff.

I know, I know.

But to my disappointment she repeatedly refused. Finally I asked, "Why not?"

"Well," she said, "someone might look at it fifty years from now and think it was a three-generation photo."

To my sorrow, our chance to make merry was gone—until about twenty years later, when my relatives from Indiana were coming to my home in Virginia for a family event. One night two weeks before, I had an idea. "How fun would it be," I thought, "to secure a photographable chimp and redeem that lost opportunity from years ago!"

In short order I found one, and on the appointed day, when I saw the chimp and her handler coming up our sidewalk, I told my mom, "Put on some lipstick. I have a surprise for you!"

She was all excited this time, and for ninety unforgettable minutes, we were engaged in a primal frolic with this little ape— slightly scary since, by the end of our time together, we were all acting pretty much alike.

The sweetest moment of the day, however, was when my mom and I at long last sat down for our photo with a chimpanzee.

Sometimes God encourages us to chase after joy, tapping us on the shoulder, saying, "Hey, this is worth the pursuit! Go for it!"

A PRAYER

Dear God, please show me how to rearrange my life for the sake of joy and, unafraid of chasing down your abundance, celebrate the call of the wild in my soul.

50

Make the Ordinary Joyful

Take your everyday, ordinary life—your sleeping,
eating going-to-work, and walking-around life—
and place it before God as an offering.

—Romans 12:1 MSG

Injecting joy into our ordinary lives can be a challenge, since this would involve placing an infinite list of unexciting tasks before God and saying, "Here. For you from me."

And that list includes house cleaning, laundry doing, grass cutting, errand running, and dinner cooking.

It helps to spend time with someone who can work up a crazy dose of enthusiasm over what, to most folks, is a fairly ordinary task. I found such a person on a PBS showing of vintage Julia Child videos. I couldn't stop watching this lady who was endlessly enthusiastic about all things culinary.

In one show, she made bouillabaisse, and I'm telling you, the woman was fearless. Such joy she took in whacking (with something that looked like a hatchet) the heads off some fish. Then she jubilantly threw the other smaller fish into the pot with their faces on. She also showed us how to skin an eel, and then tossed him into his brothy grave. The result: a big cauldron of boiled fish stew, which she placed on the table, then tucked a giant napkin into her shirt and dug in with all the exuberance of a kid jumping into a pile of Twinkies.

On another episode, as the theme song for *The French Chef* played, you could see Julia doing a little jig in the background. Her exuberance was contagious, and I came away a little more enthused about my own time in the kitchen.

What would happen, then, if you asked God for a little inspiration from someone who enjoys doing a task you find just plain unremarkable?

You just may know a friend who, like Julia, can help you transform the everyday into the exceptional and the ho-hum into the holy.

A PRAYER

Dear God, please show me—maybe through a friend— how to find the sacred in the mundane and offer it all back to you with a grateful heart.

51

Say Yes

It is God who works in you, both to will
and to work for his good pleasure.
—Philippians 2:13 ESV

When I first saw the movie *Chariots of Fire*, I was inspired by Eric Liddell's giftedness as a runner and even more enchanted by his words, "When I run I feel God's pleasure."

How magnificent would it be, I thought, to feel God's pleasure in a parallel universe of endorphin-induced euphoria?

But when my friend Beth invited me to train for a 10K, my first inclination was to say, "No way," since I'd never run anything close to that distance before.

Over the next couple days, however, visions of Eric Liddell kept dancing in my head. So eventually I said yes.

As it turned out, training was excruciating. But when race day arrived, I actually galumphed my way through the entire ten kilometers.

I was excited later to go online and look up photos of myself. In my mind I had morphed into a gazelle. But when I found my picture, I noticed a telling detail: there was a girl in the picture who was passing me on the left. She was wearing a yellow bib. Yellow bibs were for walkers.

Yes, folks, this woman was walking faster than I could run. But, oh well.

Because somehow, even at my limited skill level, I was feeling God's pleasure.

Probably because God was laughing. But whatever. All good. Better than good, actually.

So maybe you are more of a "no" person, a bit more prone to resist when God presents you with a crazy little idea. But saying yes just might open up your spirit, enlarge your world, and even inspire more joy than you imagined.

A PRAYER

Dear God, when you offer an invitation to delight, please nudge me to say an exuberant "Yes!" and feel your smile on me.

52

Do What Makes You Come Alive

God will let you laugh again; you'll raise
the roof with shouts of joy.

—Job 8:21 MSG

My friend Alison lost her grandfather and her father very suddenly at the same time. I played the music for that devastating double funeral, and I worried about the family's response to this tragedy in the days following. But Alison told me their story of coming alive:

"My brother decided that after the really hard stuff was over, it might be nice to have a day of laughter—because that is what Dad would have wanted. And where do people go when they want to laugh and have a good time all day long? Well, King's Dominion [an amusement park], of course!

"I honestly didn't know how Grandma would feel about it since we wanted to go the day after she buried her husband and her son. But she was all about it!

"At the park we rode rides and took turns sitting with her. But my favorite part of the day was when we passed the carousel, and Grandma said, 'You know, I think I could handle that.'

"So we all got on the carousel, and I remember looking at her, smiling and laughing on her bobbing horse. And I was so grateful to be alive with her in that moment.

"It was a good day. We needed to remember my dad and my grandpa, and we needed to remember we were still here and we could still laugh."

Did this family's grief disappear during a trip to an amusement park? Of course not. But they could find life by filling their day with a kind of joy that helped them breathe and even smile. Like the apostle Paul, they discovered what it meant to be "immersed in tears, yet always filled with deep joy" (2 Corinthians 6:10 MSG).

How has God wired you to come alive, friend? Would you consider letting him resurrect your soul, even in the toughest of times?

A PRAYER

Dear God, please show me your power to bring life to my darkest days.

53

Learn from a Mess-Up

Blessed are those who find wisdom,
those who gain understanding.

—Proverbs 3:13

I honestly didn't know I'd made an illegal U-turn until the police officer enlightened me.

An unsympathetic judge in court gave me two options: pay the fine or go to traffic school. I chose the latter.

The "school" was run by two ladies (I'll call them Thelma and Louise), whose job it was all day long to force us to view one very old videotape after another about the dangers of drivers using CB radios and bag phones.

At one point, I looked around the room to see how my fellow prisoners were holding up. They had gone from catatonic in the morning to comatose in the afternoon, draped all over the furniture in various states of unconsciousness.

But at the end of the day, I was all the wiser for eight hours in that instructional abyss, because I learned that this driving school was not about instruction. It was about punishment: detention for adult teenagers from 8:30 a.m. until 5:00 p.m.

And because of that little adventure, I will never, ever make an illegal U-turn again.

What about you? Have you ever blundered in a way that makes you say, "I'll never do that again," or chided yourself with thoughts like, "What was I thinking?"

We have a tendency to berate ourselves for our mistakes, but consider this: Now you are wiser than you've ever been before. And God can use that wisdom—in the form of a smarter you providing perspective to someone else who needs it right now. Not to mention the entertainment value of a good story around a fire pit.

A PRAYER

Dear God, please help me learn from my own mistakes, and show me how to pass along my new wisdom to a friend in need of encouragement.

54

Work on Your Worry

Can any one of you by worrying add a single hour to your life?
—Matthew 6:27

When our daughter, Jamie, moved to Boston she insisted on making the flight alone and setting up her apartment with help from nobody. The "nobody" would include her parents. I took her picture in the dark as she left early that morning, and I may or may not have hustled directly into the house to throw up.

We understood. Some things you've got to do on your own. It's a challenge, though, when your baby goes off to a strange place alone.

In the beginning we talked to her every evening. It eased my mind a little, but one night at the usual call time, she didn't answer. I was highly agitated. Ben, of course, said something rational, like, "She probably just went to bed early."

"At 8:30?" I said, incredulous. "And she keeps her phone right by the bed! How could she not hear it ringing?"

Further down the worry pit I fell, imagining every horrible scenario possible.

Of course I prayed and asked God to help me trust Him. I finally went to bed around midnight, actually able to trust Him until I woke up at 3:30 a.m., heart pounding, eyes wide open, and checking my texts to see if she had answered. Nope.

Finally, to reassure me, Ben called her at 5:00 a.m. She was fine. She'd—yes—gone to bed really early the night before.

What do you worry most about, friend? And how do you stop it?

No easy answers here, but it might help to think about what you'd say to a loved one in this dilemma. Then, of course, you'd best talk to your calmest friends—of the mere mortal kind, and also the Divine.

A PRAYER

Dear God, you know everything I'm worried about. Please help me turn my anxieties and cares over to you, as your Word tells me to do (1 Peter 5:7). And in return, please send me your peace and wisdom and the calm of a trusted buddy.

55

Leave a Sticky Note

Let us consider how we may spur one another
on toward love and good deeds.
—Hebrews 10:24

On a trip to New York City, my friend, author Tamara Letter, stopped at a little café and penned encouraging words on sticky notes to place around the city. After writing messages such as "You are loved," she left the notes on bathroom mirrors, gift shop shelves, subway seats, and inside books.

Always prepared, she now carries a "kindness caddy" everywhere, stocked with pens and sticky notes.*

Everyone needs affirmation, and this kind can be mighty indeed. And you don't have to personally know the recipient of your note of encouragement.

After author and artist Liv Lane was diagnosed with an aggressive form of cancer, she found that writing sticky notes and placing them at random places around the Mayo Clinic helped relieve her anxiety. At the same time, messages such as "Wishing

---

*Tamara's book, *A Passion for Kindness: Making the World a Better Place to Lead, Love, and Learn* (San Diego: Dave Burgess Consulting, 2019), is an uplifting and practical guide to the power of kindness in an increasingly unkind world.

you a day of good answers and great care" brought joy and solace to patients and caregivers.*

One of the most anxiety-laden spaces for me is the dressing room where patients prep for mammograms. The note I found there one day that said, "You're beautiful!" not only made me smile but inspired me to leave similar messages in that space every time I visit.

Friend, where do you find yourself in the company of people going through a difficult time?

Where do you find *yourself* during a difficult time?

Because leaving notes in places of particular need—*if you happen to be sharing that need*—might make it extra special, placing them anywhere folks are desperate for encouragement.

A PRAYER

Dear God, please make me aware of opportunities to put a sticky little message of joy into someone's day . . . or night.

---

*Liv Lane, Instagram, January 22, 2022, https://www.instagram.com/p/CZQO3BxMYqf.

56

Tell Me Something Good

Give thanks to God—he is good.

—1 Chronicles 16:34 MSG

Focusing on something good in the middle of your current craziness can spawn a whole lot of joy.

Easier said than done, you may say, and you're absolutely right.

But if your soul is spiraling downward, here's one way to give it a set of wings: every day, take a picture of something good that happens in your life, and put each picture into a photo journal that you make for just a week, a month, a year, or a season—especially a difficult season.

During a challenging time in my life, when I decided to make my own journal, I was at a conference in a fancy hotel. But it wasn't the building's exquisite design that most impressed me.

It was the bathroom in the lobby. Not because of its beautiful decor, although that was more tasteful than my living room.

It was the music.

I walked into this space expecting a fairly utilitarian atmosphere, and instead got Vivaldi. And Mozart. And Chopin, which instantly created some high-class ambience. I was absolutely transported.

So of course I took a picture of the stall I was in to remind myself of the charming ear candy in a surprising place. I could hardly wait for that pic to claim a spot in my photo journal.

Maybe you'd like to make such a journal yourself. And yes, there are apps for that. But years from now, long after you've put your five thousand pictures on a zip drive and thrown the thing in a desk drawer to be ignored for a long, long time, your little album will be there on your nightstand to send you to sleep with a mind and heart focused on the goodness of God.

A PRAYER

Dear God, thank you for reminding me of the very small treasures that each day holds—sometimes where I least expect them.

57

Bring a Clown

Do to others as you would have them do to you.
—Luke 6:31

Few would argue the benefits of having people around to give you emotional and physical support.

The challenge here is rustling up a willingness to summon these people into action when you require assistance.

Why don't we—maybe you—ask for support when we clearly need it?

Maybe you don't want to bother anyone with your challenges. Maybe you believe that calling in reinforcements indicates that you are somehow inadequate. Maybe you're an "overgiver," feeling as though you can only be a good person if you always pour out and never ask to be filled up.

But friend, God created you for connection with humans and designed you with a desire to feel supported. You're part of the body of Christ, which is designed with God's intention that "all the members care for each other" (1 Corinthians 12:25 NLT).

So the next time you need to be propped up, you might follow the crazy lead of Josh Thompson from New Zealand. One day when he got a letter from his bosses requesting a meeting, he knew he was about to be fired from his job. In New Zealand, employees are allowed to bring along a support person to such a meeting to cushion the blow. But instead of bringing a friend or family member, Josh hired a clown named Joe to accompany him. As Josh was being fired, his support clown was making balloon animals and faking tears.*

It did add a much-needed touch of humor to the office that day, and Josh says he highly recommends hiring a cheer giver.

If not a clown, would you consider inviting a trusted someone to help you navigate a difficult season? We all need encouragers, and God gives us to each other for this reason.

A PRAYER

Dear God, thank you for the people in my life who will walk with me through hard times. Please help me remember that it's okay to lean on them.

*"New Zealand: Man Brings Clown to Redundancy Meeting," *BBC News*, September 15, 2019, https://www.bbc.com/news/world-asia-49708570.amp.

58

Do Love

As I have loved you, so you must love one another.
—John 13:34

Often love is more verb than noun. So exactly how does love act?
Sometimes love protects.

During a visit to New Orleans with friends a few years ago, we decided to take a swamp tour on an airboat—a flatboat powered by a gigantic fan in back.

The guide knew the alligators by name, and they knew him by voice, so when the boat cruised through the gatorhood and stopped, one named Dominique paddled out to the boat looking for all the world like a Labrador retriever.

She was, however, on the opposite side of the boat from me, and I was trying to get a good picture. So I got up to jump onto the good side, forgetting that my seat was on a little platform, and bam! I fell down. The people on the boat heard the thud and later said they'd waited half a dreaded second for the splash. Apparently everyone was prepping to rescue me from the clap-happy jaws of Killer Dominique.

Fortunately, I had fallen onto the boat, not into the water. But when I got up, Ben was resuscitating his own heart. The rest of the day he practically glued himself to me, never more than an inch away, never letting me out of his sight.

That's what love does when the person you love has a propensity for disaster.

Love also . . .

bakes cookies.

sends a text.

gets up early.

stays up late.

forgives over and over.

Love holds tight. Love lets go.

Love changes diapers on babies . . . and adults.

Love carries a bag of groceries—or any load that might be too heavy for one person.

Love gives life.

No wonder Jesus set the example, and then said, in so many words, "Your turn. Go make it a verb."

A PRAYER

Dear God, please show me every time when I can "do" the love someone needs today.

59

Lean into God

I am the LORD your God who takes hold of your right
hand and says to you, Do not fear; I will help you.

—Isaiah 41:13

My friends and I were on a ski trip, attempting to learn how
to look cool on the slopes.

Mainly, though, we had wobbled our way down every hill,
spending much of the day falling backward, lurching forward,
and keeling over sideways.

One night we decided it was time to give our bodies a break,
and were clomping around in our ski boots, trying to get from
the main lodge to our bunkhouse. It was dark, so we couldn't
detect the expansive sheet of ice that covered the parking lot we
were trying to cross.

As you would expect, we were continually slipping, sliding,
and crashing to the ground. It was funny at first, but at one point
my backside was getting weary of the abuse.

Suddenly I was startled to feel an arm around my shoulders.
A park employee had seen us struggling and had come over to
help. Somehow sure-footed on that glassy surface, he held me up
and said, "Just relax. I've gotcha." When I finally leaned into his
strength, I could trust him to get me to the other side.

And I will never forget, in the middle of my clumsiness, how it felt to be held up in the darkness.

That night I couldn't help but think, "Feels like God."

Sometimes He lets us crash and fall, over and over.

I don't know why.

But somehow, when night falls, He's always there, His arm around us, with an invitation to trust Him to get us across the most treacherous territory.

A PRAYER

Dear God, when I'm bumbling around in the dark parts of my life, please remind me that you are waiting to help if I'll only lean into your strength.

PART FOUR

The Best of Life

60

Offer Comfort

The LORD is good, a stronghold in the day of trouble;
he knows those who take refuge in him.

—Nahum 1:7 ESV

Sometimes God lets us land in an undesirable place just to bring solace to someone else.

Once when Ben and I were on a road trip, rains flooded the highway and forced us off the exit to a little town, where the police herded us to the local high school gym for shelter.

We were thankful, but as the day dragged on we became pretty agitated, especially when the Red Cross arrived. That's when we realized we were about to live an introvert's nightmare: a big ol' group sleep, nose to nose with one hundred strangers.

Fortunately, the Red Cross provided cots and food.

Unfortunately, they did not provide clean underwear.

One lady, traveling solo, asked if she could set up her cot next to ours. She was on her way to see her mother in hospice care. Ben and I, and the family on the other side of her cot, did our best to surround her.

The second evening, when we saw her in distress on her phone, we rushed over.

"I tried to get to her, but my mother died without me," she wept.

All we knew to do was pray with her and comfort her with our words and our presence.

Late that night the National Guard bounded in, yelling, "If you want to leave, you've got to get out NOW!" Bridges were washing out and dams were breaking. So we rushed out, following our friend onto the highway.

As we watched her taillights disappear, we asked God for safe travels for her and her sorrowing spirit.

Such a brief encounter. But we'll always believe He placed us beside her to bring comfort as she realized she wasn't alone.

A PRAYER

Dear God, please show me how I can come alongside a fellow traveler and offer a hand and some heart.

61

Hand Out Some Kindness

Therefore, as we have opportunity, let us do good to all people.
—Galatians 6:10

My friend Sandy and I like to dress up—not in a classy Audrey Hepburn way but more like in a whimsical Ronald McDonald way. Sandy has been a clown. I've done time in a cow suit.

Of course, then, Halloween is a favorite holiday. We think it's a fine excuse to costume oneself.

One year, however, nobody was inviting us to their parties.

So, undeterred, we had an idea. Knowing so many people who had been through challenging times that year, we thought, "Why not do a *reverse* trick or treat?" We would dress up, but we'd *give out* treats rather than show up at their door with an open pillowcase. It would be a small way to use our wiring to initiate a little adventure in kindness.

Sandy put our outfits together (we were Lucy and Ethel in

the candy factory),* and off we trotted—for two nights, since we had too many names to cover in one. Most of the time, we didn't just stand at the door, we went in and chatted for a while. Shared smiles and news. Gave out treats.

The following years we morphed into Minnie Mouse, then Wonder Woman. When people were isolating during a pandemic, we were masked flamingoes, flocking a lot of yards with ourselves. True, we couldn't venture up close. But we learned that just the sight of joy brings joy—even at a distance.

So how has God wired you for delight? Could you tap into whatever brings you cheer, then find a way to share it with someone who's struggling right now?

A PRAYER

Dear God, I know that people are desperate for the life-giving power of a warm heart. Please show me how to use my joy to spread joy to them.

*Lucy and Ethel were the feature characters in the hugely popular 1950s sitcom *I Love Lucy*, whose reruns have continued to be aired in the United States and across the world. For a good laugh, check out this clip from the chocolate factory episode on YouTube in the black-and-white original: https://www.youtube.com/watch?v=AnHiAWlrYQc. (A colorized version also exists.)

62

Say "Thank You"

I thank my God in all my remembrance of you.
—Philippians 1:3 NASB

I once received an email that changed a corner of my life. That same email could very well change yours too.
It said,

Hello Jill Baughan,

My name is Bill Roberts and I'm not selling anything or asking for any donations! I was a student of yours at VCU [Virginia Commonwealth University]. I have the greatest memories of being in your class.

As we move through life we meet lots of people, and sadly some pass away and all we have are memories of them. I've had a few close friends come to the end of their lives recently. Thinking back about people who have touched me, I remembered you and your endless support and kindness.

I'd love to speak to you and to say thanks for the great VCU memories!

Do I need to tell you how moved I was by the fact that Bill took the time and effort to say thank you?

Bill realized we just don't have time to delay thanking people for the ways they have touched our lives. And he remembered a simple little English class and its teacher.

So he and his wife met my husband and me for dinner one night, and we spent a totally delightful couple of hours catching up on the last thirty-six years.

But that's not all. He inspired me to go looking for people from my own past to thank, so I began a list and embarked on my own gratitude adventure.

Ephesians 4:29 says, "Let everything you say be good and helpful, so that your words will be an encouragement to those who hear them" (NLT). Is there a teacher, a friend, or even an acquaintance from your past you need to thank? If so, please know that your words of gratitude could lift them even higher than they lifted you.

A PRAYER

Dear God, please bring to mind someone from my past who was a light to my path, and show me how to offer the thanks that person deserves but never got from me.

63

Share a Healing Experience

He comes alongside us when we go through hard times,
and before you know it, he brings us alongside someone
else who is going through hard times so that we can be
there for that person just as God was there for us.

—2 Corinthians 1:4 MSG

Eric Evans was struggling with grief after his wife, Jaime, died. They ran an alpaca farm, and after her passing, the alpacas helped him process his sorrow.

So he started hosting events, introducing people to the healing power of animals. At one experience he met Katie, who later became his fiancé. When he gave her four baby goats, they began offering classes in goat yoga to people struggling with loss, trauma, and mental illness.*

I could not resist their story and a chance to frolic with goats for an hour, so my cousin Emily and I signed up.

*Terrence Dixon, "Hanover Farm Brings Goat Yoga to Central Virginia." *WBBT 12 On Your Side*, June 21, 2022, https://www.nbc12.com/2022/06/21/hanover-farm-brings-goat-yoga-central-virginia/. See also Goat Yoga RVA, website, accessed August 4, 2024, https://goatyogarva.com.

In about five seconds we found out if you get on all fours, you will have a goat on your back in short order. We fell in love with this exuberant play, and we weren't alone. Hundreds of folks in need of comfort and support can now find it in the place where Eric and Katie found it themselves.

So how about you? Is there a way you could share—with someone who's struggling—an experience that God used to helped you heal?

Maybe you found comfort in the outdoors and could invite a friend for a hike. Maybe you found peace in coffee and conversation.

Maybe you could lend your heart as you walk someone to another side of their pain.

A PRAYER

Dear God, please help me remember what filled my soul on my own road to healing, and show me how to share that experience with someone still on the journey.

64

Be Open to Adventure

Every good and perfect gift is from above.
—James 1:17

Our family was in Alaska with friends, looking forward to a kayaking trip to a glacier. The day dawned cloudy and drizzly, however, and as we reached the launching point, the guide gave us the sad news: "No kayaking today; the weather won't cooperate." The tour company then offered us one alternative: a four-hour bus tour of Juneau.

We were sure Juneau was a perfectly nice city, but we had been primed for a little more adventure. Disappointed, we gathered around to decide our next steps when a vision of hope caught my eye: a young lady with a hand-lettered cardboard sign that said, "Zip line."

We weren't sure it was a legitimate business, but it couldn't hurt to check it out, right?

After a van ride and a short hike to the middle of nowhere for an information session, our twelve-year-old instructors (okay, they looked twelve to me) suited us up and addressed our concerns.

Mostly I was worried about being suspended in midair, twirling around in circles on a cable like Tarzan gone wild. But after the practice run, knowing that a twelve-year-old was waiting at the next tree, ready to absorb the impact of my arrival if needed, I was relaxed and ready to go.

We then zipped over a mile through the breathtaking Alaskan rainforest, thanking God for this trip through the most exquisite sanctuary ever.

Sometimes God surprises you with an opportunity for adventure. It may be a departure from your plans, but it's worth considering that so often He might be offering you an even more joyful gift than you could imagine.

A PRAYER

Dear God, thank you for happy surprises. Please help me stay open and alert for your invitations to remarkable experiences.

65

Watch for Magnificent Moments

You make known to me the path of life; you
will fill me with joy in your presence.

—Psalm 16:11

Magnificent moments often take you by surprise and fill you with joy—like accidentally finding an extraordinary treasure in the middle of an ordinary day, sometimes in a most unlikely place. Such occasions expand your vision beyond your current troubles, and they transport you—not away to escape, but back in touch with your heart. The expansive part of your heart, not the breaking part.

Trying to engineer magnificent moments is tricky business. Just catching them, however, can result in joy of the highest order.

My mom and I were celebrating her ninety-seventh birthday at the mall. We were tooling our way toward a big department store when I spotted a tempting sight: Santa in all his rotund glory, sitting on his throne, surrounded by wonder and elves. He was giving Mom the eye.

And when Santa gives you the eye, you must respond.

"Hey Mom!" I said. "It's your birthday! Let's go get your picture taken with Santa!"

Askance was how she looked at me, but I knew I had momentarily lured her into my brand of shamelessness. She sidled up to the jolly old elf, then sat down and laughed harder than she had in a long time.

I had a Christmas ornament made of that photograph for everyone in the family. Every year when I hang it on the tree, I smile and thank God for a way to celebrate that precious memory over and over.

Each new day brings potential for magnificent moments. Too often, though, they can slip by unnoticed if we're not walking around with watchful hearts.

A PRAYER

Dear God, I want to embrace every fleeting, extraordinary opportunity for joy you provide. Please wake me up to your life-giving wonder every day.

66

Take a Second Opportunity for Joy

Be very careful, then, how you live—not as unwise but
as wise, making the most of every opportunity.
—Ephesians 5:15

When I was five years old, I thought any day that included a polio shot had to be the worst day ever.

I was so wrong.

After that traumatic visit to the doctor, my mom and I stopped at the Kroger store, and there in the parking lot I caught sight of it with my delighted eyes: the Oscar Mayer Wienermobile—redemption in all its wienery glory. My day was officially made.

Almost.

I wanted to go inside for a look around, but alas, we were not allowed. So after a superficial examination of that ginormous Oscar Mayer ad, we left (but at least with my very own wiener whistle).

Decades later, though, on an ordinary Saturday of running errands, what should catch my eye but a modern-day version of the same official Wienermobile.

Of course my husband and I stopped to investigate and jumped in line—because this time not only were we allowed to explore the shiny red-and-yellow insides, but we could participate in creative photo ops, sticking our heads through cardboard cutouts of hot dogs and ketchup squeezers.

All in a Kroger parking lot.

Oh, the full-circleness of it all!

Sometimes, friend, God gives you a second chance at joy. It may be as fun and superficial as doing something in adulthood that you never had the opportunity to do as a child but wanted to. Then again, it may involve restarting a relationship, taking a trip, or serving a group of people when the opportunity comes around again.

A PRAYER

Dear God, please alert me to opportunities for joy today that may have passed me by previously. I understand that they may or may not involve a wiener whistle, and that is okay.

67

Make Friends with Annoying

Praise Him with tambourine and dancing; praise
Him with stringed instruments and flute.

—Psalm 150:4 NASB

Once at a concert, three young people sat in front of Ben and me: a pretty girl and two guys. One was obviously her boyfriend; the other poor fellow she flirted with occasionally so he wouldn't feel like a fifth wheel.

Apparently the girl's raison d'etre that night was to revel in jumping up and down, throwing her arms around her boyfriend and occasionally around Fifth Wheel.

Now, I'm all about enthusiasm at concerts. But these people were right in my sight line, making it impossible to see the band. I wanted them to go away so I would have an unobstructed view of the stage.

Because, of course, the concert was all about me.

When they started taking selfies, I just rolled my eyes. But then, for reasons known only to God, my heart softened, and I asked myself, "Can you just make friends with this situation? These people?"

And suddenly, what I *wanted* to do was stick my head between Jumping Girl and Fifth Wheel just in time for the camera click.

But I didn't.

Because I might have looked even goofier than they were acting. Or they might have been hostile or thought I was crazy or—worst of all—old. (Too late to worry about that one.)

You too have probably had the opportunity to make friends in annoying, inconvenient circumstances. Maybe with a person who crosses your path. Maybe even with the circumstances themselves. Or both.

Personally, I am now sorry I didn't follow my soul's prompting and photobomb the Three Mouseketeers in front of me.

Because maybe we would have talked with each other. We probably would have actually liked each other.

I promise I'll find out next time. Maybe you will too?

A PRAYER

Dear God, making friends with annoying people is not my gift, so please remind me that you might connect us in unexpected ways—in joy, even.

68

Invite God into the Day

In the morning, LORD, you hear my voice; in the morning
I lay my requests before you and wait expectantly.

—Psalm 5:3

Is your morning routine soul sucking?

Author Tish Harrison Warren was disturbed to realize that her morning habit of immediately reaching for her smartphone imprinted her day with technology, so she changed her routine. Sometimes she'd read Scripture. Sometimes she would pray.

"But mostly," she says, "I'd invite God into the day and just sit. Silent. Sort of listening. Sort of just sitting. But I sat expectantly. God made this day. He wrote it and named it and has a purpose in it."*

Inviting God into the day can be life giving—however you do it.

For me, it's taking a shower. In this sacred space, a refuge from the rest of the world for a few minutes, I ask Him into whatever the next twenty-four hours hold. When I come out, I feel more awake. Refreshed. God oriented.

It's like church without the people.

*Tish Harrison Warren, *Liturgy of the Ordinary: Sacred Practices in Everyday Life* (Lisle, IL: InterVarsity Press, 2019), 28.

How about you? Does your morning routine alert you to all that happened in the world overnight without you? Does it point your mind toward too many tasks on your calendar? Does it remind you of a lack, a sorrow, a worry that you were blissfully unaware of in your unconscious state?

Instead, might you adopt a calming ritual to practice before life as you know it body-slams into your soul? You don't have to make your bed. Or even take a shower. But if it helps . . . well, you go right ahead.

And let peace of heart follow you around all day long because, as God was knocking on your bedroom door, you dragged your weary self across the room and invited Him in.

A PRAYER

Dear God, would you please show me a first-thing-in-the-morning to do that points me to joy as I focus on you?

69

Cross-Reference Some Joy

You will seek me and find me when you
seek me with all your heart.

—Jeremiah 29:13

While shopping at a party store one day, I spied an item on the shelf that made my heart beat faster: a Viking helmet—silver-painted plastic with two horns and a blonde, braided pigtail hanging from each side.

I had no idea why I felt as though I needed this headdress, but it called my name and made me laugh, so I bought it, brought it home, and put it on the shelf in the closet.

It was just about time to make dinner—a task that is neither my desire nor my gift. In the kitchen, hauling out pots and pans, I wondered, "What in the world could bring more joy to this chore?"

Then I thought about that little piece of delight in the closet. Why not combine business with pleasure? I plopped the thing on and got to work. Thus I learned that it's impossible to cook a meal with a Viking helmet on your head and not smile.

So try this: Start a running list of your personal joy producers. Post it where you can see it every day. Then when you're facing an undesirable life event, choose something from that joy list to walk beside the unpleasantness.

Waiting in line? Look at pictures on your phone that make you happy.

Waiting for test results? Play music that lifts your spirits.

Worried about a family member? Take a walk in the woods.

Stressed about work? Play with some children you love.

Pair the undesirable with the delightful, my friend. It's a day changer.

A PRAYER

Dear God, thank you for a way to access extraordinary in the unsavory parts of life. Help me remember I can find you, the source of joy, walking beside me in all the tough stuff. Always.

70

Make Yourself Uncomfortable

Let your light shine before others.
—Matthew 5:16

Have you ever had the opportunity to do something a bit risky but life changing? Or at least day changing?

Just a few years ago, unbeknownst to her, my mom's granddaughters were concocting a scheme to ramp up the social life of their ninety-four-year-old Grandma Mary.

After perusing an old photo album and collecting a few names, they found one of her old flames, ninety-six-year-old George, who lived only forty-five miles away and was game for a visit from her.

"Ohhh, no," she said, resisting. "He might think I'm trying to start something."

After some cajoling, however, she relented, and we escorted her to George's home, where he ushered us to a table loaded with photos. For two hours we listened to the two of them call up priceless days.

When we had to go, we gathered at the front door. Mary looked up at George and said softly, "I'm glad we came."

Pause. (We all leaned forward, expecting a little Hallmark movie action.)

And then she said, "I just want you to know that this whole thing was *not* my idea."

Because, of course, she didn't want him to think she was trying to start something.

Sigh.

But on the way home she was smiling with a very present gladness about the risk she had just taken.

So what about you?

Is God nudging you to do something risky that would bring some joy to the world? Put your faith in motion (James 2:22). Maybe someone needs you to say, "I appreciate you." Maybe you need to reach out to an old friend. Maybe you need to use a gift you have to encourage someone instead of letting it lie dormant because you'd rather play it safe than share.

Maybe now is the time to make yourself uncomfortable.

A PRAYER

Dear God, please help me be brave enough to follow your lead into unfamiliar territory, so together we really can "start something"!

71

Find Joy in Grief

I will turn their mourning into gladness; I will
give them comfort and joy instead of sorrow.

—Jeremiah 31:13

When my mom passed away, my brother, Ted, and I wanted
to be sure to invite joy to her memorial service.

Our first task was to put together a little brochure. We needed
a photo.

"I have an idea," said Ted, "but it might be inappropriate."

I knew exactly what he was thinking, and I jumped on board.
The photo we put on her brochure was one of her and a charming
chimpanzee, taken years before in a raucous moment that made
the whole family smile.

Then we had decisions to make about music. I wanted to play
the piano before her memorial service, and one night I had an
inspired thought: Why not, in addition to her favorite hymns,
include a medley of Greatest Generation songs? After all, it was
the music of her life.

Granted, this notion was a little risky, since people at my home
church weren't accustomed to hearing songs like "Boogie Woogie
Bugle Boy" at a funeral. But my brother and I thought it was a

fine idea, so we made prelude plans that included "Chattanooga Choo Choo," "In the Mood," and "Sentimental Journey."

And oh, the joy on that day of sorrow!

When the music concluded, people applauded. Exuberant, wonderful applause. Not for the musician but for the way the tunes lifted hearts and made people sing inside themselves (and sometimes outside) as thanks to God for this lady who lived such a long, remarkable life.

At the end of the service, we exited in celebration to "Stompin' at the Savoy."

It kinda made me want to dance—to pull the shroud off my grieving heart and set it free.

Finding joy in grief can do that for you.

A PRAYER

Dear God, please show my heart how to discover great, unorthodox delight even in times of great pain and loss.

72

Ask for Help

The task is too heavy for you; you cannot do it alone.
—Exodus 18:18 NASB

Are you someone who's reluctant to ask for help?
I understand.

When I broke my leg and people asked, "What happened?" I was too embarrassed to say, "I fell off a bike." Instead I told them, "I had an unfortunate encounter with the pavement while I was working out."

At first, wrangling crutches was just frustrating. Then maddening.

I ran into stuff. I tripped over stuff. I dropped stuff. I was slow. And clumsy.

In the beginning, I was reluctant to ask for help with anything (even though I needed assistance with almost everything). I didn't want to inconvenience the people around me, but it didn't take me long to realize that most folks actually love to help someone in need.

A gentleman finished pumping my gas one morning.

Friends carried my jacket, hauled my books, shouldered my backpack.

Lots of people opened doors for me.

Granted, I found there *are* people who will watch you try to open a door *with your head* (true story)—but so many more will sprint across a parking lot to give you a hand.

And as a result of cultivating a new habit of saying, "Yes, thank you," I now know this: when we let someone else help us, we create an environment that is ripe for joy—times two! There's the joy that comes from being helped as well as the joy that comes from helping, since God hard-wired us to lend a hand or some heart when we encounter someone in need.

So. Where do you need help now—physically, emotionally, or some other way?

Please ask, and know that you just might make someone's day by doing so.

A PRAYER

Dear God, when I start thinking I can do this life alone, would you please just help me get over myself?

73

Listen to Good Advice

The way of a fool is right in his own eyes, but
a person who listens to advice is wise.

—Proverbs 12:15 NASB

A friend once gave me wise advice while I was still learning to navigate the world on crutches: "Whatever you do, when you're going down stairs, don't lean forward."

Early on I did quite well—until one day, when I paused at the top of our stairs at home to get my bearings. With both crutches locked into my armpits, I leaned forward a little too much . . . just enough to launch me into the point of no return.

It was a very fast worst-feeling-ever when all I could see for a second was a set of uncarpeted wood steps coming at my face. I shudder to think about it even now.

I yelled so my husband could hear my voice one last time as I was most likely on my way to meet Jesus.

Then I thunk-rolled down the entire flight of stairs until I landed at the bottom—glasses bent up, one lens out and flung to the outer limits of our entryway.

Ignoring good advice often has a price.

Maybe you already knew this.

Maybe, before your brain had finished growing, you

stuck a jellybean up your nose anyway.

touched a hot stove anyway.

drove too fast anyway.

And even now, when your brain is fully adult but not always inclined to wisdom, maybe you should consider taking the good advice of a trusted someone who says something like

"You should ask a doctor about that," or

"Don't try to do this alone," or

"Please call me when you feel like that."

Because following good advice can actually be a good idea.

A PRAYER

Dear God, thank you for sending me people with sense. Please help me listen and heed wise words when I'm poised to descend into disaster.

74

Search the Inside of a Hard Story

My God turns my darkness into light.
—Psalm 18:28

What can we do to find joy when suffering makes no sense? Sometimes we have to look for it in the middle of a big, bad story.

In April 2020, at age ninety-one, my much-loved father-in-law, Arthur, contracted COVID-19 and was taken to the hospital.

Like so many families, we were heartbroken that we couldn't see him in person.

We talked to him on the phone often as his condition kept declining. He struggled to breathe, and after just a few days in the hospital he choked out the words to us, "I'm ready to go."

But we weren't ready to let him go.

Because, you see, he was an imperfectly delightful human being who ended every conversation he had with Ben with a nod to me: "Tell her she's beautiful."

And for him to die alone . . . it wasn't fair.

But. There was a nurse. Her name was Karen.

She video-called us regularly from her own phone, masked and suited up, continually stroking his head with a gloved hand, risking her own health to speak comforting words to him.

We said our goodbyes, then watched while she held her phone so we could see, as the time between breaths got longer. And finally, when his chest failed to rise, Ben said, "I think he's gone."

Karen listened to his heart with her stethoscope and nodded. And she cried with us.

It was the most terrible, beautiful thing I've ever seen.

And we will forever thank God for this precious nurse.

You too may find yourself in the middle of an awful time. If so, it might help to look for light, even there.

A PRAYER

Dear God, when my suffering makes no sense, please help me find comfort in knowing that inside every awful big story you plant many smaller stories of peace, beauty, compassion, and even joy.

75

Lament

How long must I wrestle with my thoughts and
day after day have sorrow in my heart?
—Psalm 13:2

When I was in middle school, I really enjoyed a good foray into misery. I kept a diary which, to be honest, exactly nobody would want to read, but it was important to me, full of disquietude and angsty adolescent ramblings.

Then I grew up and grew much less inclined to vent my distress; however, I have since learned that lament needs expression.

Author Barb Roose says, "The only way toward health and healing is to embrace grief, fully feel it, and then learn the practice of releasing it back to God."

She periodically does this through an exercise she calls an "emotional funeral."

Every year, for one day, she takes her Bible, a blanket, a notebook, and some tissues to a nearby beautiful river and in her notebook lists all the unanswered prayers, unmet expectations, and unfilled dreams that have died in her life.

"The sentences in my notebook," she says, "begin with phrases such as, 'I really hoped,' 'I wished,' 'I truly thought,' or 'I prayed so hard that . . .'"

Then she reads a few verses of hope from her Bible and prays an "ugly-cry prayer," surrendering to God the things that will not be.

Over the past decades of having an annual funeral, Barb has learned that "when I let go of my dead dreams, God plants new ones in the fertile soil of faith that has formed as I fought in prayer for those dying dreams or desires."*

Friend, may you too feel free enough to express your lament over what isn't, and engage in your own form of releasing your sorrow to make room for joy.

A PRAYER

Dear God, thank you for your permission—even encouragement—to give my heartache expression and space.

*Barbara Roose, "Do You Need to Have an Emotional Funeral?," September 13, 2021, https://barbroose.com/do-you-need-to-have-an-emotional-funeral/.

76

Embrace Imperfection

We know that for those who love God all
things work together for good.
—Romans 8:28 ESV

High school reunions sometimes have a pretty sketchy repu-
tation, but as my fiftieth approached, I was determined to
make the scene after all those years.

I carefully chose my outfit because, I'll be honest, I wanted to
look good. I wanted people to lie to my face and tell me I hadn't
aged at all since 1972. Thus I had plans for my clothes, hair, and
anti-aging makeup.

However.

My flight was delayed the night before. I missed my connection and couldn't arrive until 11:30 the next morning. Since the
event started at noon, I thought, "Okay, I'll change clothes, make
up my face in the airport bathroom, and just go directly to the
reunion. No worries."

My flight came in right on time.

But my suitcase did not.

My suitcase with my kicky outfit, my makeup, and my hair
products was sitting somewhere in Detroit, mocking me from

afar. And the airline, insensitive to the urgency of my dilemma, said that it would not arrive until that evening.

So I had no choice but to go to the gala in my jeans, athletic shoes, and crazy, unwashed hair.

But once I made my entrance—to my delight—nobody cared. Not a bit. As it turned out, our good time was not about how good we looked; it was, instead, about present joy.

Of course we talked about the past, but the best part of the reunion was in discovering who we'd become. No one in the room had arrived unscathed by life, and sharing the challenges, the troubles, and the bumps in our roads made the day that much more beautiful.

Good news: You don't have to wait for a big reunion to appreciate your own dented-up God story. The dents are an indispensable part of its beauty—and you never know where and when someone might need to hear it.

A PRAYER

Dear God, please show me how to celebrate the beauty you can bring in the middle of my imperfect life.

77

Ask God What to Do

The Lord will guide you always.
—Isaiah 58:11

A chipmunk was running wild in our house.
I assumed there was nothing to do but get a broom and wait for a brazen appearance. Sure enough, in just a couple minutes he came strolling out from under the couch like he owned the place.

Immediately I jumped up and chased him all over the living room. Finally, face-to-face with him on a chair, I raised the broom to knock him senseless.

But he was frozen in fear, looking at me with big pleading eyes, his tiny, terrified body atremble . . . and I just couldn't do him in. Laying down my weapon, I reluctantly trudged upstairs to bed, hoping he'd grow some sense overnight and leave.

The next morning, though, I spied him in the kitchen—back against the wall between the cabinets and refrigerator, fast asleep.

I (and this is important) asked God for wisdom. You know—as in, "If any of you lacks wisdom, you should ask God . . . and it will be given to you" (James 1:5).

He sent me to YouTube.

With the help of a couple of videos, I decided to put some cat food into a plastic grocery bag, set it in front of the space where he was snoozing, creep into the next room, and wait for him to come and get it.

No more than sixty seconds later, I heard the rustling of plastic, came into the kitchen, picked up the bag, peered into the bottom, and came face-to-face with those big pleading eyes again. This time, though, it was my pleasure to take him outside and set him free at last.

Friend, whether the challenge is life threatening or just a little ridiculous, it's important to ask God for some guidance. He may do a direct deposit into your head, or He may lead you to another resource. Either way, He will guide you to the next step.

A PRAYER

Dear God, I'm in need of some direction right now. Please help me hear your voice and feel your hand showing me what to do.

78

Act in Faith

We walk by faith, not by sight.
—2 Corinthians 5:7 ESV

Sometimes, when you take a leap of faith, God nods His head and says, "Yes!" Sometimes He shakes that same head and says, "No. Not now." And sometimes, "No. Not ever."

Acting in faith can be exhausting.

When our daughter called one day in tears to say, "I think I had a miscarriage," my heart broke for her and her husband. Immediately I decided to start a journal of prayers for the next baby to come.

I struggled with the notion that maybe this was just my own wishful thinking; nevertheless, I felt God leading me to start writing out prayers for this child who had yet to be conceived. In a year, she gave birth to a baby boy, and I couldn't wait to tell him, "I loved you before I knew you."

Two years later it all happened again: a happy pregnancy announcement, and then a text that said, "No longer pregnant. Can't talk now."

Once more I felt God leading me to start another journal of prayers for another baby-to-be. And when she eventually gave birth to another little boy, I couldn't wait to tell him too, "I loved you before I knew you."

God used the prayers in those journals to create bonds with my grandsons before they were born. But here's the truth: the point of my trusting God was not that we got the happy ending we wanted. Because, I assure you, the presence of the ultimate joy did not negate the sorrow that became a permanent part of us along the way.

My *hope* was for a happy ending, but my (often faltering) *faith* was in a God who hears and comes near.

May it be so for you too.

A PRAYER

Dear God, please help me be unafraid to act in faith, knowing that, whatever the outcome, you are surrounding my fragile heart always.

79

Go to Plan B

We humans keep brainstorming options and
plans, but GOD's purpose prevails.
—Proverbs 19:21 MSG

For a long time I've dreamed of dog sledding in the snow.

It hasn't exactly happened yet. At least not the way I pictured it in my overactive imagination.

But a few years ago in the fall, we were in Stowe, Vermont, when I saw an advertisement for four-season dog sledding. At first I dismissed the information because I thought if there were no snow, it wouldn't be the stuff of my Iditarod dreams. However, I was curious, so I called.

In warmer months, the owner said, they use wheels instead of runners, and run the sleds through the woods. It sounded like fun. No snow, true, but I was quickly emerging into a Plan B mindset that could quite possibly be as much fun as my Plan A.

When we arrived at the property, the owner ushered us into what was obviously the dogs' living room. At the sight of us, they sprang to life, and in a hot minute we were covered up with canines.

Then when the owner yelled, "Let's go!" all the dogs shot off toward the door, yelping and jumping like there was a side of beef waiting for them outdoors.

"These animals love to mush," he said as we jumped into the sled and went for a wild, beautiful ride through the New England countryside—snowless but dripping with vibrant fall foliage.

Sometimes Plan B can be just as amazing as Plan A.

Maybe you've been forced onto an alternate path you never anticipated.

But hear this: Plan B just might create an opportunity and offer surprises that bring a kind of joy you never imagined.

A PRAYER

Dear God, when I'm forced onto a path I didn't choose, please help me call a truce with circumstances beyond my control and stay alert for another way to experience your delight.

80

Do What You'll Regret Not Doing

Do not fear, for I am with you; do not be dismayed,
for I am your God. I will strengthen you and help you;
I will uphold you with my righteous right hand.

—Isaiah 41:10

Days after her husband died, ninety-year-old Norma Bauerschmidt discovered she had uterine cancer. Doctors prescribed surgery, chemotherapy, and radiation, but her son and daughter-in-law, Tim and Ramie, gave her another option: join them in their motor home, traveling the country to spend the remainder of her days exploring places she'd never been.

"I'm ninety years old," Miss Norma said. "I'm hitting the road."

And that's exactly what they did for over a year, traveling to every state but Alaska. When they started a Facebook page documenting their escapades, people from all over the world responded. They asked her to dinner, made her the guest of honor at their celebrations, let her ride in parades, and gave her tours of cities and ships.

It wasn't always easy. There were constant concerns about her health and safety. But with every new experience, Norma became bolder and more open to adventure. So did Tim and Ramie.

Then something even more remarkable happened. People gathered their families and took trips that they'd been putting off. They told those who mattered to them "I love you" for the first time. Residents in nursing homes began to choose life in their final days.

Thus, the adventure of Norma, Ramie, and Tim became way bigger than the three of them.*

So what about you?

What might you regret not doing? Remember, God may want to bless other lives if you'll only accept His offer to bless yours.

A PRAYER

Dear God, I don't want to live a life of regret over what I didn't do. Please show me how to reach in faith for the fullness you want to give me.

*Tim Bauerschmidt and Ramie Liddell, *Driving Miss Norma: An Inspirational Story about What Really Matters at the End of Life*, reprint ed. (New York: HarperOne, 2018).

81

Ride On

*I will instruct you and teach you in the way you should
go; I will counsel you with my loving eye on you.*

—Psalm 32:8

Years ago in Santa Fe, I saw a picture of an old cowboy who
had been knocked off his horse. Underneath him was this
sign: "Ain't been throwed? Prob'ly never rode."

There's comfort in them there words.

Case in point: One day while canoeing on the Shenandoah
River, my husband and I learned that sometimes getting a little
heave-ho can yield some valuable information.

The ride went something like this:

> Me (the lookout in the front): "HEY! ROCKS!"
> Him (the rudder in the back): "WHERE?"
> Me: "THERE!"
> Him: "AHHHH!! You have GOT to tell me
> before they're SIX INCHES AWAY!"
> Me: "Go RIGHT!"
> Him: (canoe turns like the Titanic) "I'm doing
> the BEST I CAN!"

Me: "AHHH!
GORIGHT-GORIGHT-GORIGHT!"

We of course slammed into the rocks, then flipped over into the rapids going crazy under us.

Ben stood up and grabbed my hand, but I submerged, the current forcing my head underwater. I couldn't get to my feet and slid back under the rushing water, coming up gasping for air a second time, a third time. Then a fourth.

Finally I struggled to stand, and Ben led me to a nearby boulder, shouting, "Sit! Stay!" like I was his dog. We were glad to be alive, but still pretty irritated with each other for causing the accident.

Not our finest hour, but we learned it's helpful to treat such unfortunate events not as failures but, rather, as reconnaissance, the gathering of information. Our most valuable discovery that day: we needed kayaks. One-person, can't-blame-disaster-on-your-partner kayaks.

Surely, friend, you too have been "throwed" by some joy-stealing life challenge.

But surely you too emerged, a little roughed up but with some useful information.

So it wasn't all for naught. At least you rode.

And that might be just enough for joy.

A PRAYER

Dear God, please teach me what you want me to know when it all goes wrong. And thanks for the ride.

180

82

Ask God into Physical Pain

Come to Me, all who are weary and
burdened, and I will give you rest.
— Matthew 11:28 NASB

Ever been in pain?

Maybe you're in pain right now.

If so, you will understand that . . .

Pain makes you angry.

Pain makes you tired—physically and emotionally.

Pain is depressing. One time, on a bad day with my own pain, I pointed to my head and said to someone, "I need you to understand, it's dark in there."

Pain makes you dread getting out of bed in the morning because when you wake up, your first thought is, "Ugh. Another day of struggle."

Pain inspires you to snap at someone trying to help you.

You want to talk about it. Then you don't want to talk about it because you don't want to bore people, and anyway, you're sick of talking about it.

Pain takes over your spirit, and you just don't know why God is allowing it. If it's to "teach you a lesson," you are most willing to learn it and *move along*. But no, it drags on, starting out like a pesky fly that eventually evolves into an albatross flapping around your head, making you blind to everything but itself.

Unfortunately, we can't always make our pain disappear.

But we can ask God to enter into it.

Author Sarah Bessey, when recovering from a debilitating accident, discovered the importance of "simply joining with God to care for ourselves as a mother would care for us . . . a wise, capable, strong, patient, kind, no-nonsense, deeply loving mother."

"Sometimes," she says, "the answer has been simply: 'Take a nap, child. I've got you.'"*

A PRAYER

Dear God, when I am circling the drain, everything hurts, and my mind and spirit are going dark, please come into my pain and "fluff my pillow" the way only you can.

---

*Sarah Bessey, *Miracles and Other Reasonable Things: A Story of Unlearning and Relearning God* (New York: Howard Books, 2019), 170.

83

Take a Nap

When you lie down, you will not be afraid; when
you lie down, your sleep will be sweet.
—Proverbs 3:24

Some people have no nap-shame.

They are excellent at taking naps, and gift themselves whenever they feel the need. For instance, my father-in-law could fall asleep just about anywhere, just about any time.

One day he took his wife to K-Mart and decided to wait for her in the car at the curb. In short order he was snoozin' away.

Until he heard a tap-tap-tap on his car window.

It was a police officer, informing him of his illegal parking and maybe illegal napping.

He probably got a good ten minutes of sleep in, though, which, according to some sources, can be rejuvenating—for Arthur, enough to get him to the next store.

Others of us feel a little embarrassed about taking a nap, even if we desperately need one. No need for that, though. Much research shows that short naps during the day can increase productivity and reduce stress.

And often when you need a nap, nothing else will do.

One time in college I was extra tired from working a job and taking a full course load. In the library I told myself that I would just "lay my head down" on a desk for a minute. The next thing I knew, another student was tap-tap-tapping me on the shoulder. I raised my head and squinted at him, wondering for a split second where I was. "Are you all right?" he asked. "I walked by here two hours ago, and you haven't moved. I thought you might be dead."

Apparently that was some nap. And I was some kind of tired.

Jesus knew that sometimes what His followers needed most was a little rest (Mark 6:31). So be not ashamed to joyfully give in to your God-ordained duty to take your heavy eyelids—and your health—seriously, my friend.

A PRAYER

Dear God, thank you for smiling on my sleep. Please help me honor my body's needs whenever I can.

84

Decorate Your Rogue Anatomy

She is clothed with strength and dignity;
she can laugh at the days to come.
—Proverbs 31:25

After two hip replacements, I was grateful for relief from pain. But when I discovered I then required a knee replacement, I needed serious consolation. So I told myself, "Well, it could be worse. At least I don't have cancer."

Oops.

Two years later, after receiving positive test results from a breast biopsy, I learned that you cannot unring that bell in your head and your soul. And one bad day, I stood in the middle of our bedroom and announced to my husband, "I despise my body." My words startled even me.

But my body was not behaving in an acceptable manner, and I was over it.

You know how that feels. It doesn't have to be terminal to be life altering.

It may be a broken bone, a food allergy, or a slow metabolism.

Sometimes it's a disease; sometimes it's a germ. Other times, it's just parts misbehaving, formed wrong, all whacked out.

It's when your body frustrates you or frightens you or feels like it's not your friend.

So I decided on one way to deal with body betrayal: decorate that thing.

I went to my next radiation appointment in a crazy pair of tiger-print leggings. As soon as the radiologist saw them she exclaimed, "Oh I love those!" So I started wearing wild britches to every hot date with the linear accelerator machine in order to generate some sunshine in that room . . . and beyond.

Maybe you could do the same, adding a little jazz to your uncooperative body and a little joy to those around you.

A PRAYER

Dear God, there may be no answer to the issues of my rogue anatomy. But would you show me how to decorate it and generate some light in someone's darkness today?

85

Get Physical

You shall love the Lord your God with all your heart and with all your soul and with all your mind and with all your strength.

—Mark 12:30 ESV

How would you describe your high school phys ed experience? Some folks had a great time; others, however, found this class a place where awkwardness and bullying thrive. (Dodgeball, anyone?)

Athletic prowess was not one of my gifts. I was fairly clumsy and proficient at zero sports, so I spent my freshman year feeling like an uncoordinated loser in gym class.

Since then, though, I have discovered that, although not all of us are athletes, God created us as physical beings, and there is much joy in moving your body—whatever your preferences or even your ability.

Consider Sue Austin, confined to a wheelchair, who realized one day that scuba gear extends your range of activity in the same way that a wheelchair does. "So I thought," she said, "I wonder what'll happen if I put the two together."[*]

*Sue Austin, "Deep Sea Diving . . . in a Wheelchair," TEDxWomen 2012, filmed in December, 2012, YouTube, https://www.ted.com/talks/sue_austin_deep_sea_diving _in_a_wheelchair?language=en.

And thus the underwater wheelchair was born, taking her on an amazing journey as she glided in her chair, exploring ocean beds, and floating free in 360 degrees.

Sue is not a traditional athlete. Yet she is inspiring other people to get physical—in their own way.

What about you? If you have a restriction, though it may not be as dramatic as Sue's, it is not so limiting that it can't be viewed through a different lens.

It might look like showing up at therapy, stretching outdoors, breathing deeply, or chair dancing from the waist up.

Just moving your body can nourish your spirit. You don't need a playbook (though if you've got one, great!). You don't need a triathlete's drive. All you need is a little determination—just enough to make it happen.

A PRAYER

Dear God, thank you for the joy of moving my body. Would you show me some creative ways to get physical?

86

Celebrate Now

For everything there is a season, and a time for every
matter under heaven. . . . A time to weep, and a time
to laugh; a time to mourn, and a time to dance.

—Ecclesiastes 3:1, 4 ESV

Carolyn had the unparalleled opportunity to party at her own
funeral before she died.

As her pastor, James Lamkin, put it, "We knew Carolyn was
dying. And we knew it would be sooner rather than later. We
knew our grief would be immense."

So her faith community decided, with her permission, to have
a celebration of her life while she was still alive.

They booked a Dixieland band, brought in food, and formed
a receiving line that gave each person a chance to hug Carolyn
and speak to her.

The highlight of the day, however, was when her husband of
fifty-four years asked her to dance. Though she was weary in
body, she accepted his hand as the band played a slow, soulful
rendition of "Just a Closer Walk with Thee." And as friends,
family, and faith community applauded, says Reverend Lamkin,
"I'm not sure if time collapsed or expanded. But I'm reasonably
certain that linear time stopped, and vertical, eternal time began.

"Grace made space and time parenthetical. . . . It was an out-of-time, beyond time, moment."*

When Carolyn died, her community did indeed cry buckets. But no one regretted celebrating her while she was still with them.

How can you do the same, recognizing the joy in front of you today, even though today might be full of uncertainty or sorrow?

A PRAYER

Dear God, even when there is much to grieve, please show me ways to celebrate your gifts that are before me now.

---

*James Lamkin, "The Last Dance," originally published on December 16, 1996, in the newsletter of the Ravensworth Baptist Church, Annandale, VA.

87

Make a Life List

Commit to the LORD whatever you do,
and he will establish your plans.

—Proverbs 16:3

You're probably familiar with the concept of a bucket list—a manic pursuit of adrenaline rushes in order to beat the clock that's headed toward your death. To summon more joy into your life, however, might you consider a change in terminology? What if, instead, you were to make a life list of adventures that teach you how to live?

One item had been on my list since childhood: to ride on the back of a convertible in my hometown street fair parade. From childhood to adulthood, I dreamed of being a contender for queen, all dressed up with a sash across my front that stated my title of Miss Something or Other.

Then once upon a time, during my brother's final year as mayor, he was asked to be the grand marshal and ride in a horse-drawn carriage in the parade with my sister-in-law. When they asked if I would like to join them, visions of the pageant wave started dancing in my head. So of course I said yes.

And it was amazing. For a few minutes I forgot everything that was wrong in the world, because riding in a fancy horse-drawn carriage in a hometown parade, waving wildly at people you know, is surreal in a most remarkable way.

Yes, there were jokes about the carriage turning back into a pumpkin. And I get it. The parade ends, and poof! No more bibbidi-bobbidi-boo.*

Maybe.

But maybe not.

Because that was better than a thousand rides on the back of a convertible with a Miss Behavior sash across my chest.

So how about you? What would be on your own life list? Would you be willing to log a few dreams and make your list a catalyst for soul-filling joy?

A PRAYER

Dear God, how I'd love to experience this kind of aliveness. Please lead the way.

---

*If you're not familiar with that phrase, you've obviously never watched the 1950s Disney animation *Cinderella* . . . and you should. Oh, yes, you should, definitely.

Be Spontaneous

I'm whistling, laughing, and jumping for joy;
I'm singing your song, High God.
—Psalm 9:2 MSG

The summer I broke my leg, my sister-in-law and I were visiting a gigantic music store. She was pushing me in a wheelchair to preserve my energy when we rolled past an unexpected surprise—a towering spiral slide that started on the second floor and descended all the way to the first. What a great alternative to boring old stairs!

When I spotted it, I shouted, "Marge! Look!"

"I want to slide so badly, but I guess it's out of the question with this brace on my leg," I complained. But of course, neither of us found that flimsy excuse acceptable. We knew we had to carpe diem* and ride this joyful surprise.

It was a little tricky, but we figured it out. Marge pushed my chair into the elevator, and we rode up to the second floor, then went to the top of the slide. I got out of the chair, hopped over on my good leg, then set my hind parts in the "go" position. When I was ready to launch, Marge ran with the chair to the elevator

*"Seize the day," in case Latin isn't your second language.

and rode to the first floor to the bottom of the slide. After she gave me the thumbs up, I pushed off and sailed, broken leg in the air, all the way down.

At the bottom, I hopped to the chair, and waited for Marge to dash up the stairs and slide down herself. Then we did it all again several times.

Oh, the exhilaration of an impulsive joy ride!

True, we could have believed the lie that making a few adjustments would be too much trouble. But we would have missed the best play of the day.

A PRAYER

Dear God, I would love to embrace more spontaneity. Please help me feel your hand on my back, pushing me just enough to send me sailing into joy.

89

Stick a Little Umbrella in It

Rejoice always, pray without ceasing,
give thanks in all circumstances.
—1 Thessalonians 5: 16–18 ESV

"Hey," I said to myself one summer. "Let's kick off a fun July Fourth weekend with a colonoscopy!"

Well, okay, it didn't exactly happen like that. I was due for this treat, we were going to be in town where the hospital was, and I wanted to get it over with.

What I dreaded most wasn't even the procedure; it was the prep, which generally involves drinking what feels like gallons of liquid designed to clean your clock, so to speak.

And as I was girding up my psychological loins for this process, I thought, "Okay, Joy Lady, you need to figure out how to add some positive to this party."

I tried to think about whatever lifts my spirits, so I cued up a little tropical music. Wearing my sunglasses and a beach hat, I mixed up my celebratory libation, then dug around the pantry and found the ultimate symbol of a warm-weather good time: I stuck a little umbrella in it.

Then, "Cheers and bottoms up!"

I'd be lying if I said that this made the whole process fun; however, it flavored an undesirable process with a little joy—joy that would not have existed had I not been intentional about looking for a bit of levity in a less-than-fun event.

So. Maybe you could do the same the next time your life takes you somewhere unpleasant—and, let's be honest, that'll probably be soon. To be clear, we're not talking about tragedies here, just a state of affairs that makes you say to the Lord, "Oh, I'd rather not." Of course you wouldn't. But as long as you're here, you might as well start a party.

A PRAYER

Dear God, I am this minute thinking of an "I'd rather not." Would you help me find a way to stick a little umbrella in it and toss some joy into the mix?

90

Know That Joy Is Here

You have made known to me the paths of life;
you will fill me with joy in your presence.

—Acts 2:28

I was once at a basketball banquet catered by a restaurant chain whose mascot, a person in a cow suit, bounded in, high-fiving kids and cavorting all over the gym in fun fashion.

"Ooh, I could do that!" I thought. So the next time I was in the restaurant, I asked the manager, "What exactly does it take to play around in the cow suit?"

"A pulse," he said.

So after I applied and was awarded the job of "area market cow," I was blessed to perform five times in that getup. At one event, I was waiting to go on when I felt my hormonal furnace revving up, sending the temperature inside that already sweltering suit into the stratosphere.

"Oh, please no, God!" I pled, but not just because of the heat.

Since Ben and I had dealt with infertility for most of our married life, every one of my personal summers was a sign that my reproductive years were coming to an end, and "No more babies" was God's final answer.

You too know what it feels like when God says no, and it

doesn't make any sense. But at that particular moment of escalating temperatures, God in His wisdom gave me a revelation that revolutionized my perspective.

"Wow," I thought, "this is a perfect picture of joy and sorrow in the same place—me having a hot flash in a cow suit!"

I had to laugh, and that moment became a reminder that it's possible for joy and sadness to walk side by side in the same life.

It's just up to us to access the joy while we're going through hard times.

A PRAYER

Dear God, please help me find my own version of a cow suit to remind me that joy is here, all around me. No matter what.

Spread the Word
by Doing One Thing.

- Give a copy of this book as a gift.
- Share the QR code link via your social media.
- Write a review of this book on your blog, favorite bookseller's website, or at ODB.org/store.
- Recommend this book to your church, small group, or book club.

Connect with us.

Our Daily Bread Publishing
PO Box 3566, Grand Rapids, MI 49501, USA
Email: books@odb.org

Love God. Love Others.

with  Our Daily Bread.

Your gift changes lives.

Connect with us. 𝕗 ⃝

Our Daily Bread Publishing
PO Box 3566, Grand Rapids, MI 49501, USA
Email: books@odb.org